BUENC

TRAVEL GUIDE

2024 Edition

The Ultimate Traveler's Guidebook to Crafting Unforgettable Memories in the Heart of South America

Roxanne azure

All rights reserved. No part of this book may be reproduced, stored in a retrieval system, or transmitted in any form or by any means, electronic, mechanical, photocopying, recording, or otherwise, without the prior written permission of the copyright owner. The information contained in this book is for general information purposes only. The author and publisher make no representations or warranties of any kind, express or implied, about the completeness, accuracy, reliability, suitability or availability with respect to the book or the information, products, services, or related graphics contained in the book for any purpose. Any reliance you place on such information is therefore strictly at your own risk

Copyright © 2023 by Roxanne Azure

Table of Contents

Introduction	**7**
Chapter 1	**9**
Getting Started	*9*
A Brief History	9
Best Time to Visit	12
Visa and Entry Requirements	14
Vaccinations and Health Precautions	18
Basic Essential Phrases	22
Essential Packing Checklist	25
Budgeting and Money Matters in Buenos Aires:	29
Optimizing Your Duration of Stay in Buenos Aires	34
Chapter 2	**41**
Discovering Buenos Aires	*41*
Neighborhoods Unveiled	41
Architectural Marvels in Buenos Aires	44
Parks and Green Spaces in Buenos Aires: Urban Oases of Tranquility and Recreation	48
Chapter 3	**53**
Transportation Options	*53*
Arriving in Buenos Aires: Airports	53
Navigating Within Buenos Aires	54
Additional Transportation Tips	56
Chapter 4	**59**
Accommodation options	*59*
Luxury Escapes in Buenos Aires	59
Top Boutique Hotels in Buenos Aires	61
Top Bed and Breakfasts in Buenos Aires	64
Top Guesthouses and Inns in Buenos Aires	67
Top Rentals in Buenos Aires	70
Budget-Friendly Lodgings: Top Hostels in Buenos Aires	73

Chapter 5 — 77

Outdoor Experiences in Buenos Aires — 77
- Exploring the Eclectic Parks and Green Spaces — 77
- Water Adventures along the Rio de la Plata — 78
- Thrilling Urban Adventures — 79
- Biking Adventures Through the City Streets — 80
- Aerial Adventures: Paragliding and Skydiving — 81
- Nature Retreats: Hiking and Wildlife Exploration — 82
- Safety Considerations and Tips for Outdoor Adventures — 84

Chapter 6 — 87

Savoring the Culinary Delights — 87
- Argentine Traditional Delicacies — 87
- Fine Dining in Buenos Aires — 91
- Casual Eateries in Buenos Aires — 93
- Dining Etiquette and Tips in Buenos Aires — 97

Chapter 7 — 101

Shopping Escapades — 101
- A Culinary Adventure through Local Markets — 101
- High-End and Contemporary Shopping — 105
- Discovering Buenos Aires through Souvenirs — 109

Chapter 8 — 113

Cultural immersion — 113
- Tango: The Soul of Buenos Aires — 113
- Museums and Galleries of Buenos Aires — 116
- Performing Arts in Buenos Aires — 122
- Walls of Expression: Buenos Aires' Street Art Scene Unveiled — 126
- A Cultural Mosaic of People and Language — 131
- Festivals and Events That Define Buenos Aires' Cultural Landscape — 137
- Local Customs and Etiquette in Buenos Aires — 143

Chapter 9 — 149

Nightlife and Entertainment — 149
- Unveiling Buenos Aires' Bars and Pubs — 149

  Live Music Venues in Buenos Aires   157
  Dancing into the Night: Buenos Aires' Nightclubs and Late-Night Tango Extravaganza   161

Chapter 10   167

 Practical Tips for Travelers   *167*
  Navigating Buenos Aires Safely   167
  Essential Spanish Phrases   171
  Health and Medical Services in Buenos Aires   175

Chapter 11   181

 Additional Resources for an Informed Journey   *181*

Chapter 12   189

 Conclusion   *189*
  Reflecting on Your Buenos Aires Experience   189
  Inviting You Back to Argentina   190

Important Note Before Reading

This book, "Buenos Aires Unveiled" has been intentionally crafted as a text-only guide without the inclusion of images and maps. The decision to present the information solely in written form is driven by several considerations, all aimed at enhancing the reader's experience and ensuring the utmost utility of the content.

The primary goal of this travel guide is to provide readers with in-depth, descriptive content that vividly paints a picture of the cultural richness, historical significance, and vibrant atmosphere of Buenos Aires. By abstaining from visual aids, we encourage readers to immerse themselves in the descriptive language, fostering a more imaginative and sensorial connection with the destination.

Recognizing the diverse preferences and needs of our readership, we have chosen a format that ensures universal accessibility. A text-only guide accommodates individuals with varying reading preferences, allowing them to consume the content in a way that best suits their personal learning style.

Travel information is subject to change, and the absence of static images and maps allows for more agile content updates. By relying on written descriptions, we can adapt the guide swiftly to reflect the latest developments, ensuring that readers receive the most current and accurate information available.

Omitting visual aids encourages readers to explore Buenos Aires with a sense of curiosity and discovery. By relying on textual guidance, readers are prompted to engage more actively with their surroundings, fostering a deeper connection with the destination and promoting a sense of adventure.

The absence of images and maps invites readers to rely on their imagination, allowing them to visualize the scenes described in the guide. This approach aims to spark creativity and curiosity, fostering a unique and personalized mental image of Buenos Aires shaped by each individual reader.

While we understand that visual aids can enhance certain aspects of travel guides, we believe that this text-only format offers a distinctive and immersive reading experience, allowing readers to engage more deeply with the cultural narrative of Buenos Aires. We appreciate your understanding and hope you find this guide to be a valuable companion on your journey through the captivating city of Buenos Aires.

Introduction

Welcome to Buenos Aires, a city that dances to the rhythm of tango, pulses with cultural vibrancy, and invites you to explore its rich tapestry of history, art, and passion. As the capital of Argentina, Buenos Aires is not just a destination; it's an experience that captivates the soul and leaves an indelible mark on every traveler.

Buenos Aires is a city of contrasts, where the historic coexists with the contemporary, and the bustling urban life harmonizes with serene green spaces. From the charming cobblestone streets of San Telmo to the modern skyscrapers of Puerto Madero, the city seamlessly blends its European-influenced past with its forward-looking present.

Feel the rhythm and passion of tango, the dance that encapsulates the very essence of Buenos Aires. The city's streets and neighborhoods come alive with the sultry sounds of bandoneón and the electrifying embrace of dancers. Dive into the world of milongas, where the spirit of tango is kept alive by locals and visitors alike.

Buenos Aires is a melting pot of cultures, reflected in its diverse neighborhoods and eclectic offerings. From the bohemian vibes of Palermo to the historic charm of Recoleta, each barrio tells a unique story. Immerse yourself in the city's cultural mosaic, where art, literature, and music converge to create a vibrant and dynamic atmosphere.

Indulge your taste buds in Buenos Aires, a haven for food enthusiasts. From sizzling parrillas serving up mouthwatering steaks to cozy cafes offering delectable medialunas, the city is a culinary delight. Don't miss the chance to savor traditional Argentine dishes and discover the nuances of mate, the iconic local beverage.

Buenos Aires boasts a diverse architectural landscape that showcases its storied past. Admire the grandeur of Teatro Colón, revel in the elegance of Palacio Barolo, and stroll along Avenida de Mayo to witness the city's architectural evolution. Each building tells a tale of resilience, creativity, and the ever-evolving spirit of Buenos Aires.

Experience the warmth and hospitality of porteños, the proud residents of Buenos Aires. The city's heartbeat is fueled by the friendliness of its people, who are eager to share their love for their home. Engage in conversations, join locals in their favorite haunts, and let the genuine warmth of Buenos Aires embrace you.

Buenos Aires is more than a destination; it's a journey into the heart of Argentine culture, where every corner tells a story, every note of tango resonates with history, and every taste is a celebration of culinary artistry. Get ready to be enchanted as you embark on an unforgettable adventure in the mesmerizing capital of Argentina.

Chapter 1

Getting Started

A Brief History

Buenos Aires, the dynamic capital of Argentina, has a captivating history that spans centuries, characterized by colonial legacies, waves of immigration, cultural flourishing, and periods of political turbulence. Let's embark on a comprehensive exploration of the fascinating history that has shaped Buenos Aires into the vibrant metropolis it is today.

Colonial Foundations: 16th Century

The story of Buenos Aires begins in the early 16th century when Spanish explorer Pedro de Mendoza attempted to establish a settlement named NuestraSeñora Santa María del BuenAire in 1536. However, due to conflicts with indigenous peoples and harsh conditions, the settlement was abandoned.

The city was officially founded by Juan de Garay in 1580, securing Spanish control and setting the stage for Buenos Aires to become a strategic port.

Strategic Port and Trade Hub: 17th-18th Centuries

Buenos Aires' advantageous location along the Rio de la Plata estuary positioned it as a vital port for transatlantic trade. The city's growth was accelerated by the influx of merchants and immigrants, transforming it into a bustling commercial hub.

By the late 18th century, Buenos Aires had solidified its role as a key center for commerce and cultural exchange in the region.

May Revolution and Independence: Early 19th Century

The early 19th century witnessed a period of revolutionary fervor across South America. On May 25, 1810, the citizens of Buenos Aires initiated the May Revolution, a pivotal event that marked the beginning of Argentina's quest for independence from Spanish rule.

The process culminated in the Declaration of Independence on July 9, 1816, solidifying Argentina as a sovereign nation.

Immigration Wave and Cultural Flourishing: Late 19th Century

The latter half of the 19th century marked a significant chapter in Buenos Aires' history with a massive wave of European immigration, particularly from Italy and Spain.

This influx of diverse cultures enriched the city's identity, influencing its architecture, cuisine, and arts. Buenos Aires became a melting pot of traditions and ideas.

Golden Age of Tango: Early 20th Century

The early 20th century witnessed the emergence of tango, a distinctive music and dance genre that originated in the working-class neighborhoods of Buenos Aires.

Tango's golden age, with legends like Carlos Gardel and Astor Piazzolla, solidified Buenos Aires' reputation as the birthplace of this iconic art form.

Political Turmoil: Mid-20th Century

The mid-20th century was marked by political upheavals, including the rise and fall of Juan Perón. Buenos Aires experienced periods of political instability and social unrest.

The city played a central role in the country's political landscape, contributing to its complex socio-political history.

Modernization and Globalization: Late 20th Century

In the latter half of the 20th century, Buenos Aires underwent a process of modernization and embraced globalization. The city transformed into a cosmopolitan metropolis, showcasing architectural marvels and a thriving cultural scene.

Contemporary Buenos Aires: 21st Century

Today, Buenos Aires stands as a testament to its rich and multifaceted history. The city's neighborhoods reflect the various chapters of its past, from the colonial charm of San Telmo to the modern skyline of Puerto Madero.

Buenos Aires is celebrated for its resilience, cultural diversity, and its role as a global city that continues to evolve while honoring its historical roots.

Buenos Aires' history is a living narrative that intertwines indigenous legacies, colonial influences, waves of immigration, and a relentless spirit of resilience. As you explore the streets, plazas, and landmarks of Buenos Aires, you'll discover a city that proudly wears its history, inviting you to immerse yourself in the stories that have shaped its identity. From its colonial foundations to the vibrant energy of today, Buenos Aires stands as a testament to the enduring spirit of a city that continues to captivate the world.

Best Time to Visit

Choosing the right time to visit Buenos Aires and Argentina is essential for maximizing your experience and enjoying the diverse offerings of this South American destination. This section provides a detailed guide to help you understand the best times to visit, considering seasonal highlights and local festivals.

Seasonal Highlights

Spring (September to November):

- Blossoming Landscapes: Spring brings vibrant blooms to Buenos Aires and various regions, making it an ideal time for nature enthusiasts.
- Moderate Temperatures: Enjoy mild temperatures, making outdoor activities and city exploration comfortable.

Summer (December to February):

- Festive Atmosphere: Summer is synonymous with lively festivals, beach gatherings, and outdoor events along the Atlantic coast.
- Patagonian Adventure: Explore the southern regions like Patagonia, where the milder temperatures make it perfect for trekking and outdoor adventures.

Autumn (March to May):

- Fall Foliage: Experience the picturesque autumn colors in the wine regions, providing a stunning backdrop for vineyard tours.
- Cultural Events: Many cultural festivals and events take place during autumn, offering a chance to immerse yourself in local traditions.

Winter (June to August):

- Andean Winter Sports: Head to the Andes for winter sports like skiing and snowboarding, taking advantage of the snowy landscapes.
- Cosy Buenos Aires: While Buenos Aires experiences cooler temperatures, the city takes on a cozy ambiance with fewer crowds.

Festivals and Events

Argentine Carnival (February/March):

- Colorful Celebrations: Experience the vibrant Argentine Carnival, where cities come alive with parades, music, and dancing.
- Cultural Immersion: Participate in traditional festivities, showcasing the passion and exuberance of Argentine culture.

Wine Harvest Season (March/April):

- Vineyard Tours: Visit the wine regions during the harvest season for a unique opportunity to witness winemaking processes.
- Wine Festivals: Attend wine festivals celebrating Argentina's world-renowned wines, featuring tastings and cultural events.

National Flag Day (June 20):

- Patriotic Celebrations: Join the country in celebrating National Flag Day with patriotic ceremonies and events.

- Historical Significance: Learn about Argentina's history and pay homage to its national symbols during this significant day.

Independence Day (July 9):

- National Festivities: Experience the patriotic fervor during Argentina's Independence Day celebrations.
- Parades and Events: Attend parades, concerts, and cultural events that showcase the country's pride and unity.

Choosing the best time to visit Argentina depends on your preferences and the experiences you seek. Whether you're drawn to the lively summer festivals, the autumnal colors of wine country, or the winter sports in the Andes, Argentina offers a diverse range of attractions throughout the year. Consider the seasonal highlights and local events to tailor your visit to match your interests and immerse yourself fully in the rich cultural tapestry of this captivating destination. Safe and enjoyable travels!

Visa and Entry Requirements

Ensuring you have the correct visa and meet entry requirements is essential for a smooth entry into Buenos Aires and Argentina. This section provides in-depth information on visa policies, entry documentation, and other essential details to facilitate a hassle-free travel experience.

Visa Policies

Understanding Visa Requirements:

- Argentina has varying visa requirements depending on your nationality and the purpose of your visit. Check the current

visa policies through the official website of the Argentine government or consult the nearest Argentine consulate or embassy.
- Some countries benefit from visa exemptions, allowing short stays for tourism or business purposes.

Tourist Visa:

- For most tourists, a tourist visa is not required for stays up to a certain duration. This duration can vary, so it's crucial to confirm the specific requirements based on your nationality.
- Tourist visas typically do not allow for paid work during your stay.

Business Visa:

- If your visit involves business activities, such as meetings or conferences, you may need a business visa. Check the specific requirements for obtaining a business visa, including necessary documentation.

Student Visa:

- Students planning to study in Argentina require a student visa. This involves providing documentation from the educational institution and demonstrating financial stability.

Application Process

Timely Application:

- Initiate the visa application process well in advance of your planned travel dates. Some visas may take several weeks to process, and delays could impact your travel plans.

- Check the processing times and any specific requirements for the type of visa you are applying for.

Required Documents:

- Compile all necessary documents for your visa application. This may include a valid passport, passport-sized photographs, proof of accommodation, travel itinerary, proof of financial means, and any additional documents specified by the consulate.

Visa Extensions:

- If you plan to extend your stay in Argentina, be aware of the procedures and requirements for visa extensions. Ensure that you apply for an extension before your current visa expires.

Entry Documentation

Passport Requirements:

- Ensure your passport is valid for at least six months beyond your intended departure date from Argentina. Some countries may have additional passport validity requirements.

Return Ticket and Proof of Funds:

- Immigration authorities may request proof of your intention to leave Argentina, such as a return ticket. Additionally, having proof of sufficient funds for your stay may be required.

Health Insurance:

- While not always mandatory, having travel health insurance is highly recommended. It can cover medical expenses in case of illness or injury during your stay.

Yellow Fever Vaccination:

- Depending on your travel itinerary, you may need a yellow fever vaccination. Check if your destination in Argentina is in a yellow fever risk area and plan accordingly.

Customs and Immigration Process

Arrival Process:

- Upon arrival, proceed through immigration where your visa and entry documentation will be examined. Present your passport, completed entry forms, and any additional required documents.

Customs Declaration:

- Complete a customs declaration form, declaring any items subject to inspection. Be aware of prohibited items and duty-free allowances.

Entry Stamps:

- Immigration authorities will stamp your passport with an entry stamp. Ensure that the entry stamp indicates the correct duration of your authorized stay.

Language Basics

Communication with Immigration Officials:

- While English is often spoken in tourist areas, it's beneficial to know some basic Spanish phrases. This can facilitate communication with immigration officials and enhance your overall travel experience.

By understanding and adhering to visa policies, completing the necessary application processes, and ensuring you have the required entry documentation, you set the stage for a smooth entry into Buenos Aires and Argentina. Familiarizing yourself with customs and immigration processes and respecting local regulations will contribute to a stress-free and enjoyable journey in this vibrant South American destination. Safe travels!

Vaccinations and Health Precautions

Ensuring your health is a top priority when planning a trip to Buenos Aires and Argentina. This section provides detailed information on vaccinations, health precautions, and essential tips to keep you well during your travels.

Consulting Healthcare Professionals:

Before embarking on your journey, schedule a visit to your healthcare provider or a travel clinic. Discuss your travel plans, including the regions you intend to visit in Argentina, and obtain personalized advice on necessary vaccinations and health precautions.

Essential Vaccinations:

Routine Vaccines:

- Ensure that routine vaccinations, such as measles, mumps, rubella (MMR), diphtheria, tetanus, and pertussis, are up to date.
- Verify if you need a seasonal flu vaccine based on the timing of your visit.

Hepatitis A and B:

- Vaccination against hepatitis A and B is recommended for all travelers. Hepatitis A can be contracted through contaminated food and water, while hepatitis B is transmitted through bodily fluids.

Typhoid:

- Consider getting vaccinated against typhoid, especially if you plan to explore more rural or remote areas where food and water sanitation may be uncertain.

Yellow Fever:

- Check if your travel itinerary includes regions where yellow fever is prevalent. If so, a yellow fever vaccination and an International Certificate of Vaccination may be mandatory.

Rabies:

- Depending on your activities and interactions with animals, particularly in rural areas, a rabies vaccination may be recommended.

Carrying a Medical Kit:

Basic Medical Kit:

- Pack a basic medical kit that includes essential items such as pain relievers, antidiarrheal medication, adhesive bandages, antiseptic wipes, and any prescription medications you may need.

Prescription Medications:

- If you have any pre-existing medical conditions, ensure an adequate supply of prescription medications for the duration of your stay. Include a copy of your prescriptions in case you need to refill them while abroad.

Health and Safety Precautions:

Food and Water Safety:

- Practice good hygiene, including frequent handwashing, and consume only safe food and water. Avoid street food in areas where sanitation may be a concern.

Insect-Borne Diseases:

- Protect yourself from insect-borne diseases like dengue fever and Zika virus by using insect repellent, wearing long sleeves and pants, and staying in accommodations with screens or air conditioning.

Altitude Sickness:

- If your itinerary includes high-altitude destinations, such as the Andes, be aware of the symptoms of altitude sickness. Gradual acclimatization, staying hydrated, and avoiding excessive physical exertion can help mitigate its effects.

Travel Insurance:

Comprehensive Coverage:

- Consider obtaining travel insurance that provides comprehensive coverage, including medical emergencies, trip cancellations, and evacuation. Confirm that the policy covers activities you plan to engage in, such as adventure sports.

Emergency Contacts:

- Save important contact numbers, including the local emergency services, the contact information for your country's embassy or consulate in Argentina, and the details of your travel insurance provider.

Additional Health Tips:

Stay Hydrated:

- Maintain adequate hydration, especially in the warmer months and at higher altitudes. Carry a reusable water bottle and drink purified or bottled water.

Sun Protection:

- Protect yourself from the strong South American sun by using sunscreen, wearing sunglasses, and seeking shade during peak sunlight hours.

Local Healthcare Facilities:

- Familiarize yourself with the location of local healthcare facilities in the areas you plan to visit. Carry a list of nearby medical facilities and pharmacies.

By prioritizing vaccinations, adhering to health precautions, and preparing a medical kit, you significantly reduce the risk of health-related issues during your stay in Buenos Aires and Argentina. Proactive health measures ensure that you can fully enjoy your travel experience and explore the diverse landscapes and vibrant culture of this captivating South American destination. Safe and healthy travels!

Basic Essential Phrases

Understanding and using basic Spanish phrases can significantly enhance your travel experience in Buenos Aires and Argentina. This section provides comprehensive details on language basics, including essential phrases, language apps, and cultural considerations for effective communication.

Learning Basic Spanish Phrases:

Greetings and Politeness:

- Hello - Hola
- Goodbye - Adiós
- Please - Por favor
- Thank you - Gracias
- You're welcome - De nada
- Excuse me / I'm sorry - Perdón / Disculpe

Basic Conversational Phrases:

- Yes - Sí
- No - No
- How are you? - ¿Cómoestás?
- I'm fine, thank you - Estoybien, gracias
- What is your name? - ¿Cómote llamas?
- My name is... - Me llamo...
- I don't understand - No entiendo
- Can you help me? - ¿Puedeayudarme?
- Where is...? - ¿Dóndeestá...?
- How much does this cost? - ¿Cuánto cuesta esto?

Navigating Daily Situations:

- I need a taxi - Necesito un taxi
- Where is the bathroom? - ¿Dóndeestá el baño?
- I would like to order... - Quisierapedir...
- Do you speak English? - ¿Hablasinglés?
- I'm lost - Estoyperdido(a)
- Help! - ¡Ayuda!
- I'm a tourist - Soy turista

Language Apps and Resources:

Mobile Apps:

- Duolingo: A popular language-learning app that offers interactive lessons in Spanish.
- Google Translate: An essential tool for translating text, speech, and even images in real-time.

Phrasebooks:

- Consider carrying a pocket-sized Spanish-English phrasebook for quick reference.

Language Classes:

- If time allows, taking basic Spanish language classes before your trip can provide a more in-depth understanding of the language.

Cultural Considerations:

Formal vs. Informal Address:

- In Spanish, there is a distinction between formal and informal address. Use "usted" (formal) when speaking to strangers, elders, or in professional settings, and "tú" (informal) with friends and peers.

Kissing as a Greeting:

- In Argentina, a common greeting involves a kiss on the cheek. This is a friendly gesture and is often used between friends or when meeting someone for the first time.

Patience and Respect:

- Locals appreciate visitors who make an effort to speak Spanish. Even if your proficiency is limited, demonstrating a willingness to communicate in the local language is respectful and often well-received.

Practical Tips for Language Use:

Practice Pronunciation:

- Pay attention to pronunciation, as correct intonation can significantly improve comprehension.

Use Simple Sentences:

- Keep sentences simple and use basic vocabulary to ensure better understanding, especially in informal settings.

Seek Local Assistance:

- Don't hesitate to ask locals for help or clarification. Argentineans are generally friendly and willing to assist.

Learn Local Slang:

- Familiarize yourself with some local slang or colloquial expressions, as this adds a personal touch to your communication.

By incorporating these language basics into your travel preparation, you'll be better equipped to navigate everyday situations, connect with locals, and fully immerse yourself in the rich cultural experience that Buenos Aires and Argentina have to offer. Embracing the local language adds depth to your journey, fostering meaningful interactions and creating lasting memories. ¡Buena suerte! (Good luck!)

Essential Packing Checklist

Packing efficiently is essential for a smooth and enjoyable trip to Buenos Aires and Argentina. This comprehensive checklist covers everything you need, from clothing to electronics, ensuring you're well-prepared for diverse climates and activities.

Clothing and Accessories:

Weather-Appropriate Clothing:

- Lightweight and breathable clothes for warmer temperatures.
- Layers for cooler evenings, especially if visiting during spring or fall.

Waterproof jacket for unexpected rain.

- Comfortable walking shoes for exploring the city and natural attractions.
- Swimsuit for beach destinations or hotel pools.

Accessories:

- Sun hat and sunglasses for sun protection.
- Travel-sized umbrella for rain or shade.
- Insect repellent for outdoor activities.

Formal Attire:

- A dressier outfit if you plan to dine in upscale restaurants or attend cultural events.

Personal Care and Health:

Toiletries:

- Travel-sized shampoo, conditioner, and body wash.
- Toothbrush, toothpaste, and dental floss.
- Personal hygiene items (deodorant, razor, etc.).
- Moisturizer and sunscreen.

First Aid Kit:

- Adhesive bandages, antiseptic wipes, and pain relievers.
- Any prescription medications with a copy of prescriptions.
- Insect bite relief cream.

Electronics and Gadgets:

Travel Adapters:

- Universal power adapter for charging electronic devices.

Communication Devices:

- Smartphone and charger.
- Camera or smartphone for capturing memories.
- Portable power bank for on-the-go charging.

Entertainment:

- E-reader or tablet for books or travel guides.
- Headphones for music or in-flight entertainment.

Travel Documents and Money:

Passport and Visa:

- Passport with at least six months' validity.
- Printed or digital copies of your visa and travel insurance.

Money and Cards:

- Sufficient local currency (Argentine Pesos) for initial expenses.
- Credit/debit cards, notifying your bank about your travel dates.
- Money belt or hidden pouch for added security.

Important Contacts:

- Emergency contact list, including local emergency services and your country's embassy or consulate contact information.

Miscellaneous Items:

Daypack or Backpack:

- A small backpack for day trips or carrying essentials.
- Reusable Water Bottle:
- Stay hydrated by having a reusable water bottle.

Travel Pillow and Blanket:

- For added comfort during long flights or bus rides.

Language Resources:

- Spanish phrasebook or language app for communication.

Security and Safety:

Travel Locks:

- TSA-approved locks for securing luggage.

Travel Insurance:

- Copy of your travel insurance policy and emergency contact details.

Personal Safety Items:

- Whistle, flashlight, and a small multi-tool.

Specialized Gear (Depending on Activities):

Hiking Gear:

- Sturdy hiking boots and appropriate clothing for outdoor excursions.

Beach Gear:

- Sandals, beach towel, and sunscreen for coastal areas.

Skiing/Snowboarding Gear:

- Warm clothing, gloves, and appropriate gear if visiting during the winter.

Packing Tips:

Roll Clothes:

- Roll clothes to save space and minimize wrinkles.

Ziplock Bags:

- Use ziplock bags for organizing toiletries and preventing leaks.

Limit Valuables:

- Minimize valuables, and use the hotel safe for secure storage.

Check Airline Restrictions:

- Be aware of airline baggage restrictions to avoid extra fees.

By using this comprehensive packing checklist, you'll be well-prepared for the diverse experiences that Buenos Aires and Argentina have to offer. Adapt the checklist based on the specific activities and destinations you plan to explore, ensuring a stress-free and enjoyable journey. Safe travels!

Budgeting and Money Matters in Buenos Aires:

When exploring the enchanting streets of Buenos Aires, managing your budget effectively enhances the overall travel experience. This comprehensive guide provides detailed insights into budgeting considerations, currency exchange, payment methods, and money-saving tips, ensuring you make the most of your journey without breaking the bank.

Currency and Exchange

1. Argentine Peso (ARS)

Overview:

- The official currency of Argentina is the Argentine Peso (ARS). Familiarizing yourself with the local currency is essential for seamless transactions and accurate budgeting during your stay.

Key Points:

- Coins: Centavos (subunits of the peso) come in coin denominations.
- Banknotes: Peso notes vary in value, with higher denominations for larger amounts.

2. Currency Exchange Tips

Overview:

- Currency exchange is widely available in Buenos Aires, with various options to obtain Argentine Pesos. Understanding the best practices for currency exchange helps you maximize your budget.

Key Tips:

- Authorized Exchanges: Use authorized exchange offices or banks for secure transactions.
- Compare Rates: Check exchange rates at different locations for the best deal.
- Keep Cash: Have a mix of cash for small purchases, as some places may not accept cards.

Payment Methods

1. Credit and Debit Cards

Overview:

- Credit and debit cards are widely accepted in Buenos Aires, offering convenience and security. However, it's crucial to be mindful of potential fees and to inform your bank of your travel plans to avoid disruptions.

Key Points:

- Acceptance: Major credit cards (Visa, MasterCard, American Express) are commonly accepted.
- ATMs: Withdraw cash from ATMs for better exchange rates, but be aware of associated fees.

2. SUBE Card for Public Transportation

Overview:

- The SUBE card is a rechargeable smart card that simplifies payment for public transportation, including buses and the Subte (subway). It streamlines your travel experience and helps control transportation expenses.

Key Points:

- Purchase: Buy a SUBE card at kiosks, subway stations, or authorized retailers.
- Loading: Top up your SUBE card with sufficient credit for seamless travel.

3. Cash Usage

Overview:

- While cards are widely accepted, having some cash on hand is advisable, especially for small purchases, markets, or places that may not accept cards.

Key Points:

- Small Purchases: Use cash for smaller transactions and in local markets.
- Safety: Carry a reasonable amount of cash and use secure accessories like money belts.

Budgeting Tips

1. Accommodation Costs

Overview:

- Accommodation often constitutes a significant portion of your travel budget. Understanding the range of options and factors that affect prices helps you make informed choices.

Key Tips:

- Diverse Options: Buenos Aires offers a variety of accommodations, from luxury hotels to budget-friendly hostels and apartment rentals.
- Seasonal Variations: Prices may vary based on the season, with peak times attracting higher rates.

2. Dining on a Budget

Overview:

- Exploring Buenos Aires' culinary scene doesn't have to break the bank. From traditional street food to affordable local eateries, there are plenty of budget-friendly dining options.

Key Tips:

- Street Food: Try local street food like empanadas or choripán for a quick and economical meal.
- Menu del Dia: Look for restaurants offering a "Menu del Dia," a fixed-price lunch menu that can be a cost-effective choice.

3. Transportation Savings

Overview:

- Navigating Buenos Aires on a budget is achievable, thanks to various transportation options. From the Subte to buses and walking, strategic choices help minimize expenses.

Key Tips:

- Subte and Buses: Utilize the Subte and buses for affordable and efficient transportation.
- Walking: Explore neighborhoods on foot to appreciate the local vibe and save on transportation costs.

4. Free and Low-Cost Activities

Overview:

- Buenos Aires offers numerous free and low-cost activities, ensuring you can immerse yourself in the city's culture without exceeding your budget.

Key Tips:

- Museums and Parks: Many museums and parks have free admission or discounted days.
- Street Performances: Enjoy the vibrant street performances and cultural events that often come at no cost.

5. Shopping Wisely

Overview:

- Whether you're souvenir hunting or indulging in retail therapy, shopping wisely helps you stay within budget. Explore local markets for unique finds and consider bargaining for better prices.

Key Tips:

- Local Markets: Visit markets like Feria de Mataderos for authentic souvenirs and local products.
- Bargaining: In markets or independent stores, don't hesitate to negotiate prices, especially when buying multiple items.

Buenos Aires, with its rich cultural tapestry and diverse offerings, is accessible to travelers on various budgets. By understanding the local currency, optimizing payment methods, and implementing smart budgeting strategies, you can savor the flavors, experiences, and enchantment of Buenos Aires without compromising your financial goals. This practical guide empowers you to navigate the city with financial confidence, ensuring that your journey is not only culturally enriching but also economically savvy.

Optimizing Your Duration of Stay in Buenos Aires

Determining the ideal duration of your stay in Buenos Aires is a pivotal aspect of trip planning. This guide offers comprehensive insights into factors influencing the duration, recommended lengths of stay for different experiences, and tips for making the most of your time in this captivating city.

Factors Influencing Duration

1. Trip Purpose

The purpose of your trip plays a significant role in determining how long you should stay in Buenos Aires. Whether you're on a cultural exploration, business trip, or seeking a leisurely vacation, the nature of your visit influences your ideal duration.

Key Considerations:

- Cultural Exploration: Longer stays allow for a deeper immersion in the city's cultural offerings.

Business Trip: Tailor your stay based on work commitments but allocate time for exploration.

2. Personal Preferences

Your personal preferences and travel style impact how much time you'll want to spend in Buenos Aires. Some travelers prefer a whirlwind tour, while others seek a more relaxed and immersive experience.

Key Considerations:

- Pace of Travel: Fast-paced travelers might opt for a shorter stay, while slow-paced travelers may prefer an extended visit.
- Specific Interests: Consider your interests, such as arts, history, or gastronomy, and plan accordingly.

3. Seasonal Considerations

Buenos Aires experiences distinct seasons, each offering unique attractions and activities. Your preferred season may influence the duration of your stay.

Key Considerations:

- Weather Preferences: Consider the climate during your preferred travel dates.
- Seasonal Events: Festivals, events, and outdoor activities may vary based on the season.

Recommended Durations for Different Experiences

1. Weekend Getaway

A weekend getaway to Buenos Aires provides a taste of the city's charm. While it's a brief visit, you can still experience key attractions and get a feel for the local culture.

Suggested Duration:

- 2 to 3 Days: Explore iconic landmarks, dine at local restaurants, and experience the energy of neighborhoods like Palermo and San Telmo.

2. Short Stay (5 to 7 Days)

A short stay allows for a more in-depth exploration of Buenos Aires. You can delve into cultural attractions, savor local cuisine, and experience the city's diverse neighborhoods.

Suggested Duration:

- 5 to 7 Days: Visit museums, attend tango shows, and explore neighborhoods like Recoleta, Palermo, and La Boca.

3. Extended Vacation (10 Days or More)

An extended vacation offers the opportunity to truly immerse yourself in Buenos Aires. You can venture beyond the tourist hotspots, participate in local events, and experience the city's authentic daily life.

Suggested Duration:

- 10 Days or More: Engage in day trips to surrounding areas, participate in language or cooking classes, and discover hidden gems off the beaten path.

4. Long-Term Stays (Several Weeks to Months)

For those with the luxury of time, a long-term stay allows for a profound connection with Buenos Aires. This experience is ideal for those who wish to live like a local, learn the language, and fully integrate into the city's rhythm.

Suggested Duration:

- Several Weeks to Months: Rent a local apartment, engage in cultural activities, and explore the city at a leisurely pace.

Tips for Making the Most of Your Stay

1. Prioritize Must-See Attractions

Identify key attractions and prioritize must-see locations based on your interests. This ensures you make the most of your time, even during a shorter stay.

Key Tips:

- Research iconic landmarks and prioritize based on personal preferences.
- Plan an itinerary that balances popular attractions with hidden gems.

2. Embrace Local Experiences

Immerse yourself in local experiences to gain a deeper understanding of Buenos Aires' culture. Attend cultural events, dine at local eateries, and engage with the community.

Key Tips:

- Attend tango shows, live music performances, and local festivals.

- Explore neighborhood markets and try traditional Argentine cuisine.

3. Day Trips and Excursions

Consider incorporating day trips or excursions into your itinerary to explore the surrounding areas and gain a broader perspective of Argentine culture.

Key Tips:

- Visit Tigre Delta, Colonia del Sacramento (Uruguay), or Estancias for day trips.
- Explore nearby wineries or the Paraná Delta for a unique experience.

4. Learn Basic Spanish Phrases

While English is spoken in tourist areas, learning basic Spanish phrases enhances your experience and facilitates communication with locals.

Key Tips:

- Familiarize yourself with common greetings and expressions.
- Download language apps for real-time translation assistance.

5. Stay Flexible and Enjoy the Journey

Maintain flexibility in your plans to allow for serendipitous discoveries and spontaneous experiences. Embrace the unexpected and savor the journey.

Key Tips:

- Allow time for leisurely strolls and unplanned exploration.
- Be open to local recommendations from residents and fellow travelers.

Whether you're planning a short getaway or an extended vacation, Buenos Aires welcomes you with open arms and a myriad of experiences. By considering your trip purpose, personal preferences, and the seasonal aspects of your visit, you can tailor your stay to align with your desires. This comprehensive guide equips you with insights and recommendations, empowering you to optimize your duration of stay in Buenos Aires and create memories that will last a lifetime.

Chapter 2

Discovering Buenos Aires

Neighborhoods Unveiled

Buenos Aires, the capital and largest city of Argentina, is a sprawling metropolis made up of diverse neighborhoods, each with its unique charm, history, and cultural identity. Here are some notable neighborhoods in Buenos Aires:

1. San Telmo: Historic and Bohemian

- Characteristics: Cobbled streets, historic architecture, and a bohemian atmosphere.
- Highlights: Plaza Dorrego's antique market, tango shows, and colonial-era buildings.
- Vibe: Artsy, laid-back, and nostalgic.

2. Recoleta: Elegant and Cultural

- Characteristics: Upscale, elegant streets, and Parisian-inspired architecture.
- Highlights: Recoleta Cemetery, MALBA (Latin American Art Museum), and fine dining.
- Vibe: Sophisticated, cultural, and refined.

3. Palermo: Trendy and Diverse

- Characteristics: Largest neighborhood, green spaces, and diverse sub-districts.

- Highlights: Palermo Soho for shopping and nightlife, Palermo Hollywood for restaurants and bars, and the vast Bosques de Palermo park.
- Vibe: Trendy, vibrant, and eclectic.

4. La Boca: Colorful and Artistic

- Characteristics: Colorful houses, street art, and the famous Caminito street.
- Highlights: La Bombonera stadium, artsy cafes, and tango performances.
- Vibe: Artistic, lively, and culturally rich.

5. Microcentro: Financial and Commercial Hub

- Characteristics: Central business district, skyscrapers, and historical landmarks.
- Highlights: Plaza de Mayo, the Obelisco, and iconic avenues like Avenida 9 de Julio.
- Vibe: Busy, business-oriented, and historical.

6. Puerto Madero: Modern and Upscale

- Characteristics: Former docklands transformed into a modern district.
- Highlights: Upscale restaurants, Puente de la Mujer bridge, and waterfront views.
- Vibe: Modern, sophisticated, and upscale.

7. Belgrano: Residential and Green

- Characteristics: Residential area with leafy streets and parks.
- Highlights: Chinatown, Barrancas de Belgrano park, and Embassies.

- Vibe: Quiet, residential, and green.

8. Almagro: Authentic and Local

- Characteristics: Local atmosphere, traditional cafes, and residential streets.
- Highlights: Mercado de Abasto, Corrientes Avenue, and neighborhood parrillas.
- Vibe: Authentic, local, and laid-back.

9. Villa Crespo: Trendy and Artisanal

- Characteristics: Trendy shops, artisanal breweries, and a mix of residential and commercial areas.
- Highlights: Outlet stores, leather workshops, and the Mercado de Pulgas (flea market).
- Vibe: Hip, artistic, and evolving.

10. Caballito: Family-Friendly and Traditional

- Characteristics: Residential neighborhood with parks and traditional architecture.
- Highlights: Parque Centenario, Feria de Mataderos, and historical landmarks.
- Vibe: Family-friendly, traditional, and relaxed.

Each neighborhood in Buenos Aires offers a distinct experience, making the city a mosaic of diverse atmospheres and cultural nuances. Whether you're drawn to the historical charm of San Telmo, the upscale elegance of Recoleta, or the trendy vibes of Palermo, Buenos Aires invites exploration at every corner.

Architectural Marvels in Buenos Aires

Buenos Aires, the capital of Argentina, is a city where architectural beauty meets a rich cultural tapestry. From historic landmarks that echo the city's colonial past to modern structures that showcase cutting-edge design, Buenos Aires is a treasure trove of architectural marvels. Let's embark on a journey through the city's distinctive buildings and structures that contribute to its unique skyline.

1. Teatro Colon: The Grand Opera House

- Description: Teatro Colon stands as one of the world's premier opera houses, renowned for its opulent architecture and exceptional acoustics. Designed by architects Francesco Tamburini, Victor Meano, and Jules Dormal, and later completed by J. L. White, the building's neoclassical façade conceals a lavish interior adorned with intricate details. The main hall, with its stunning chandeliers and plush seating, provides a captivating setting for performances ranging from opera to ballet.

2. Palacio Barolo: An Ode to Dante's Divine Comedy

- Description: Inspired by Dante Alighieri's "Divine Comedy," Palacio Barolo is a symbolic masterpiece designed by Italian architect Mario Palanti. The building is a testament to the fusion of architecture and literature, with each floor representing a different realm from Dante's epic poem. Ascend to the lighthouse at the top, and you'll be rewarded with panoramic views of Buenos Aires, while the building itself remains a beacon of cultural and architectural significance.

3. Obelisco de Buenos Aires: The Iconic Landmark

- Description: The Obelisco de Buenos Aires stands proudly at the intersection of Avenida 9 de Julio and Avenida Corrientes, becoming one of the city's most iconic landmarks. Built to commemorate the city's fourth centenary, this towering structure was designed by Alberto Prebisch. The obelisk's sleek and minimalist design reflects a modernist aesthetic, making it a symbol of Buenos Aires' dynamic spirit.

4. Casa Rosada: The Pink Presidential Palace

- Description: Casa Rosada, or the Pink House, is the official residence and workplace of the President of Argentina. Its distinctive pink hue comes from a mix of lime and bull's blood, adding a unique touch to its neoclassical design. The balcony of Casa Rosada has historical significance as it served as a platform for many important speeches, including those by Eva Perón. The building is a symbol of political power and cultural heritage.

5. Floralis Genérica: A Blooming Steel Flower

- Description: Situated in the United Nations Park, Floralis Genérica is a captivating steel sculpture that mimics the form of a gigantic flower. Created by Argentine architect Eduardo Catalano, the sculpture is known for its innovative design, and its petals open and close depending on the time of day. Floralis Genérica is a symbol of renewal and the transient nature of life, making it a poignant addition to Buenos Aires' public art.

6. Puente de la Mujer: Santiago Calatrava's Graceful Bridge

- Description: Designed by the renowned Spanish architect Santiago Calatrava, Puente de la Mujer, or Women's Bridge, is a striking pedestrian bridge in the Puerto Madero district. The bridge's design is said to symbolize a couple dancing the tango, an homage to Argentina's cultural heritage. With its rotating mechanism allowing it to swing open like a drawbridge, Puente de la Mujer is both a functional structure and a work of art.

7. Congreso de la Nación Argentina: Legislative Grandeur

- Description: The National Congress Building, or Congreso de la Nación Argentina, is a neoclassical masterpiece designed by architects Vittorio Meano and Julio Dormal. The monumental structure, with its impressive dome and Corinthian columns, houses the Argentine National Congress. The interior is equally awe-inspiring, featuring intricate frescoes and ornate decorations that showcase the country's commitment to democratic governance.

8. Alvear Palace Hotel: Belle Époque Splendor

- Description: The Alvear Palace Hotel is an architectural gem that exudes Belle Époque elegance. Situated in the upscale neighborhood of Recoleta, this luxurious hotel was built in 1932 and has since become a symbol of refined sophistication. The façade boasts French-inspired architectural details, and the interiors are adorned with opulent furnishings, crystal chandeliers, and timeless art, making it a haven for those seeking old-world charm.

9. Biblioteca Nacional Mariano Moreno: Literary Sanctuary

- Description: The National Library of Argentina, or Biblioteca Nacional Mariano Moreno, is a modern architectural marvel designed by Clorindo Testa and Francisco Bullrich. Its distinctive parallelogram shape and exposed concrete structure set it apart as a bold example of Brutalist architecture. The library houses an extensive collection of books and manuscripts, making it not only a visual spectacle but also a scholarly haven.

10. Puente Transbordador: An Industrial Relic

- Description: The Puente Transbordador, or Transporter Bridge, is an engineering marvel that harks back to the industrial era. Designed by English engineer A. W. Szlarek, the bridge connects the neighborhoods of La Boca and Isla Maciel. Its unique mechanism allows a suspended gondola to transport vehicles and pedestrians across the Riachuelo River, providing both a functional and nostalgic link to the city's past.

Buenos Aires' architectural landscape is a dynamic fusion of historic grandeur and contemporary innovation. These marvels not only contribute to the city's skyline but also tell the story of its cultural evolution and enduring spirit. Whether exploring the neoclassical elegance of Teatro Colon or the modernist allure of Palacio Barolo, each architectural gem invites visitors to witness the beauty of Buenos Aires from a unique perspective.

Parks and Green Spaces in Buenos Aires: Urban Oases of Tranquility and Recreation

Buenos Aires, a bustling metropolis known for its vibrant energy, is also home to a plethora of parks and green spaces that provide respite from the urban hustle. These verdant havens not only offer a breath of fresh air but also showcase the city's commitment to providing recreational spaces for its residents and visitors. Let's explore the diverse array of parks and green spaces that contribute to Buenos Aires' charm:

1. Bosques de Palermo (Palermo Woods): Urban Nature Retreat

- Description: Bosques de Palermo, also known as Palermo Woods or El Rosedal, is a vast expanse of greenery located in the heart of the Palermo neighborhood. This urban oasis spans over 400 acres and features a delightful combination of gardens, lakes, and walking paths. The Rose Garden (El Rosedal) within the park is a highlight, boasting over 18,000 rose bushes in various colors and varieties. Visitors can stroll along its pathways, enjoy paddle boating on the lake, or simply relax amid the natural beauty.

2. Parque Tres de Febrero: A Cultural and Recreational Hub

- Description: Parque Tres de Febrero is a sprawling park complex that encompasses several interconnected green spaces within Palermo. In addition to Bosques de Palermo, the park includes the Jardín Botánico (Botanical Garden), the Planetario Galileo Galilei, and the renowned Jardín Japonés (Japanese Garden). The botanical garden showcases a diverse collection of plant species, while the Japanese Garden provides a tranquil setting with traditional Japanese landscaping, bridges, and koi ponds.

3. Reserva Ecológica Costanera Sur: Nature Along the Waterfront

- Description: Situated along the Rio de la Plata waterfront, Reserva Ecológica Costanera Sur is a vast ecological reserve that offers a haven for birdwatching and nature enthusiasts. This preserved natural area spans over 865 acres, featuring wetlands, grasslands, and marshes. Visitors can explore the reserve's network of trails, spot a variety of bird species, and enjoy panoramic views of the city skyline. The reserve provides a serene escape just a stone's throw from the urban bustle.

4. Parque Centenario: A Cultural and Recreational Hub

- Description: Parque Centenario, located in the Caballito neighborhood, is a lively green space that serves as a cultural and recreational hub for locals. The park surrounds the iconic Monumento a los Españoles, and its pathways are often filled with joggers, cyclists, and families enjoying picnics. The park hosts events and performances at its amphitheater, and the nearby Natural Sciences Museum provides an educational experience for visitors of all ages.

5. Plaza de Mayo: Historic Heart and Gathering Place

- Description: While Plaza de Mayo is known more for its historical significance as the main square in front of the Casa Rosada (Presidential Palace), it also offers a green respite amid the city's historic architecture. The plaza is adorned with lush trees, providing shade for those who gather to commemorate events, express their views, or simply enjoy the surrounding greenery. The nearby Pirámide de Mayo, a historic monument, adds to the park's cultural appeal.

6. Parque Lezama: A Historic Gem in San Telmo

- Description: Parque Lezama, located in the San Telmo neighborhood, is a charming green space with a rich history. The park features walking paths, sculptures, and a gazebo, creating a serene atmosphere. The historic Russian Orthodox Church of the Holy Trinity is located within the park, adding to its cultural significance. Parque Lezama is a peaceful retreat that captures the essence of San Telmo's historic charm.

7. Plaza Francia: Artistic Flair in Recoleta

- Description: Plaza Francia, situated in the upscale Recoleta neighborhood, is a small yet vibrant square that hosts the popular Feria de Recoleta craft fair on weekends. The square is surrounded by greenery, providing a pleasant setting for visitors to explore local artisanal crafts, enjoy live music, and appreciate the surrounding sculptures. The nearby Recoleta Cultural Center adds an extra layer of cultural richness to the area.

8. Parque Avellaneda: Community Gathering in the South

- Description: Parque Avellaneda, located in the southern part of Buenos Aires, is a community-focused green space that offers a variety of recreational activities. The park features sports fields, playgrounds, and open spaces for picnics, making it a favorite among local residents. Its community center often hosts events and cultural activities, fostering a sense of community engagement.

9. Plaza Barrancas de Belgrano: Elegance in Belgrano

- Description: Plaza Barrancas de Belgrano, nestled in the Belgrano neighborhood, is a picturesque square surrounded by elegant mansions. The park is characterized by its French-inspired design, with well-manicured lawns, sculptures, and a central fountain. It provides a serene setting for residents and visitors to unwind and enjoy the architectural beauty of the surrounding buildings.

10. Parque Chacabuco: A Green Haven in the Southeast

- Description: Parque Chacabuco, located in the Balvanera neighborhood, is a spacious park that serves as a recreational hub for residents in the southeast of Buenos Aires. The park features jogging paths, sports facilities, and a lake, creating an ideal environment for outdoor activities. Its expansive green spaces provide a welcome escape for those seeking a break from the urban routine.

Buenos Aires' parks and green spaces not only contribute to the city's aesthetic appeal but also play a vital role in fostering community engagement, providing recreational opportunities, and preserving natural ecosystems. Whether exploring the historic charm of Parque Lezama or enjoying the cultural vibrancy of Plaza Francia, these urban oases offer a diverse range of experiences for locals and visitors alike.

Chapter 3

Transportation Options

Embarking on a journey to Buenos Aires is an exciting endeavor, and understanding the diverse transportation options for reaching the city and navigating within its vibrant streets is essential for a seamless travel experience. This comprehensive guide provides detailed insights into how to get to Buenos Aires and navigate the city efficiently.

Arriving in Buenos Aires: Airports

1 Ezeiza International Airport (EZE)

Ezeiza International Airport is the primary international gateway to Buenos Aires, located about 22 kilometers southwest of the city center. It serves as a hub for international flights, offering a range of facilities and transportation options.

Transportation Options:

- Taxi: Official taxi services are available at designated ranks outside the airport. Ensure you use authorized taxi services for a secure and regulated journey.
- Private Transfers: Pre-arrange private transfers for a convenient and comfortable ride to your destination within the city.
- Airport Shuttles: Shared shuttle services operate between the airport and various city locations. These are cost-effective options for solo travelers or those on a budget.

2 Jorge Newbery Airport (AEP)

Jorge Newbery Airport primarily handles domestic flights and is situated closer to the city center, making it a convenient choice for domestic travel within Argentina.

Transportation Options:

- Taxi and Ride-Sharing: Taxis and ride-sharing services are readily available at the airport for quick transfers to your accommodation or other city destinations.
- Buses: Public buses connect the airport to different parts of the city, providing an economical option for travelers.

Navigating Within Buenos Aires

1 Subte (Subway)

Buenos Aires boasts an extensive subway system, known as the Subte, comprising six lines that crisscross the city. The Subte is a rapid and efficient way to navigate key neighborhoods.

Usage Tips:

- Purchase a SUBE card for easy access to the Subte and other public transportation.
- Consult the Subte map for route planning and station locations.

2 Colectivos (Buses)

Buenos Aires features an extensive bus network, with numerous lines covering the entire city. Colectivos provide a flexible and budget-friendly means of transportation, reaching areas not served by the Subte.

Usage Tips:

- Use the SUBE card for bus rides, which can be purchased at kiosks or online.
- Check bus routes and schedules at designated stops or online.
- Queue at bus stops and wait for passengers to alight before boarding.
- Signal the driver by raising your hand when you want to get off.

3 Taxis and Ride-Sharing

Taxis are widely available in Buenos Aires, providing door-to-door transportation. Additionally, ride-sharing services like Uber and Cabify operate in the city.

Usage Tips:

- Ensure the taxi has a visible license and meter.
- Use official taxi ranks or call reputable taxi services.
- Confirm the fare estimate on ride-sharing apps before starting the journey.

4 Biking and Walking

Exploring Buenos Aires on foot or by bike is a delightful way to soak in the city's atmosphere. Ecobici, the city's bike-sharing system, offers an eco-friendly transportation option.

Usage Tips:

- Register for an Ecobici account for easy bike rentals.
- Utilize bike lanes for safe cycling.
- Wear comfortable shoes for walking explorations.

5 Car Rentals:

For travelers seeking independence, car rental companies operate in Buenos Aires. Renting a car allows you to explore both the city and its surrounding regions.

Usage Tips:

- Compare rental rates and book in advance.
- Be aware of traffic regulations and parking restrictions.
- Consider traffic conditions, especially during peak hours.

Additional Transportation Tips

1 Currency and Payment

Currency exchange is widely available in Buenos Aires. Ensure you have Argentine pesos for public transportation, taxis, and small purchases.

Usage Tips:

- Use the SUBE card for seamless payment on public transportation.
- Carry a mix of cash and cards, as not all vendors accept cards.

2 Safety Considerations

Buenos Aires is generally safe, but it's essential to remain vigilant, especially in crowded areas and public transportation.

Usage Tips:

- Keep belongings secure to prevent theft.
- Be cautious with personal items in crowded spaces.
- Use authorized transportation services for safety.

3 Language Considerations

While many in Buenos Aires speak English, learning a few basic Spanish phrases enhances your communication and cultural experience.

Usage Tips:

- Download translation apps for real-time assistance.
- Learn essential Spanish phrases for common interactions.

Buenos Aires offers a diverse array of transportation options, making it accessible and navigable for all types of travelers. Whether you prefer the speed of the Subte, the convenience of taxis, or the freedom of biking, understanding these transportation modes ensures a smooth and enjoyable journey through the captivating streets of Buenos Aires. Tailor your transportation choices to suit your itinerary, and embrace the adventure that awaits in this dynamic city.

Chapter 4

Accommodation options

Luxury Escapes in Buenos Aires

In the heart of Buenos Aires, where elegance meets cultural richness, a selection of luxury resorts and hotels awaits those seeking the pinnacle of sophistication and comfort. Here are top recommendations for indulgent stays in Buenos Aires, each offering a distinctive blend of opulence and impeccable service:

1. Alvear Palace Hotel

Location: Avenida Alvear 1891, Recoleta

- Overview: Embodying timeless luxury, Alvear Palace Hotel graces Recoleta with its historic charm and refined ambiance. Lavish suites, gourmet dining, and a commitment to personalized service make this iconic hotel a quintessential choice for discerning travelers.

2. Palacio Duhau - Park Hyatt Buenos Aires

Location: Avenida Alvear 1661, Recoleta

- Overview: Nestled in the heart of Recoleta, Palacio Duhau - Park Hyatt is a blend of classic elegance and contemporary luxury. The neoclassical palace hosts sumptuous accommodations, Michelin-starred dining, and an exclusive spa, creating an enchanting retreat.

3. Faena Hotel Buenos Aires

Location: Martha Salotti 445, Puerto Madero

- Overview: Infused with avant-garde design and theatrical flair, Faena Hotel Buenos Aires stands as a beacon of modern luxury in Puerto Madero. The hotel's decadent interiors, renowned tango shows, and upscale amenities redefine the city's hospitality landscape.

4. Algodon Mansion

Location: Montevideo 1647, Recoleta

- Overview: Algodon Mansion, nestled in Recoleta, offers an intimate escape with a blend of historic charm and contemporary indulgence. Spacious suites, a rooftop pool, and the culinary excellence of Chez Nous contribute to a refined and exclusive experience.

5. Hub Porteño by DON

Location: Rodríguez Peña 1967, Recoleta

- Overview: Hub Porteño by DON captures the essence of refined living in Recoleta. This boutique hotel provides a personalized touch with its elegant decor, spacious suites, and the culinary delights of Tarquino, making it a haven for those seeking sophistication.

Buenos Aires, a city pulsating with cultural vibrancy, opens its doors to a select array of luxury retreats. Whether immersed in the historic allure of Recoleta or the modern glamour of Puerto Madero, these top recommendations promise an indulgent escape where every moment is curated for the discerning traveler. Experience the pinnacle of Buenos Aires' hospitality in these refined havens of opulence.

Top Boutique Hotels in Buenos Aires

In the bustling heart of Buenos Aires, where history and modernity converge, boutique hotels beckon with their unique charm, personalized service, and a touch of artistic flair. Discover the intimate and enchanting accommodations that redefine luxury in Argentina's capital city. Here are top recommendations for boutique hotels in Buenos Aires, each offering a distinctive blend of character and sophistication:

1. Home Hotel Buenos Aires

Location: Honduras 5860, Palermo Hollywood

- Overview: Nestled in the trendy Palermo Hollywood neighborhood, Home Hotel Buenos Aires is a boutique gem that marries style with eco-friendly living. The hotel boasts chic rooms, a lush garden with a pool, and a tranquil atmosphere that provides a peaceful escape amidst the vibrancy of Palermo.

2. Fierro Hotel

Location: Soler 5862, Palermo Hollywood

- Overview: Fierro Hotel, situated in Palermo Hollywood, captivates with its contemporary design and personalized service. The boutique hotel features modern rooms, a rooftop terrace with a pool, and the renowned Uco Restaurant, making it a chic haven for discerning travelers.

3. Vain Boutique Hotel

Location: Thames 2226, Palermo Soho

- Overview: In the heart of Palermo Soho, Vain Boutique Hotel exudes a bohemian charm that captures the spirit of the neighborhood. The hotel's stylish rooms, rooftop pool, and the intimate Vain Club create an atmosphere of sophisticated relaxation and artistic inspiration.

4. Legado Mitico

Location: Gurruchaga 1848, Palermo Soho

- Overview: With its homage to Argentine cultural icons, Legado Mitico is a boutique hotel in Palermo Soho that embraces history and elegance. Each room is uniquely themed, reflecting the stories of legendary figures. Guests can savor the ambiance of this literary-inspired retreat.

5. Fasano Hotel Buenos Aires

Location: Posadas 1086, Retiro

- Overview: Fasano Hotel Buenos Aires, located in the upscale Retiro district, seamlessly blends sophistication with contemporary design. The boutique hotel offers luxurious rooms, a rooftop pool with panoramic views, and the renowned Fasano Restaurant for an indulgent culinary experience.

6. Nuss Buenos Aires Soho

Location: El Salvador 4916, Palermo Soho

- Overview: Set in the heart of Palermo Soho, Nuss Buenos Aires Soho is a boutique hotel housed in a beautifully restored convent. The hotel combines historic charm with modern comforts, featuring stylish rooms, a courtyard garden, and a cozy library lounge.

7. Hotel Palo Santo

Location: Bonpland 2275, Palermo Hollywood

- Overview: Hotel Palo Santo, located in Palermo Hollywood, is a sustainable boutique hotel that embraces eco-conscious living. The hotel's contemporary design, rooftop terrace with a green wall, and commitment to sustainability make it a unique and socially responsible choice.

8. Mine Hotel Boutique

Location: Gorriti 4770, Palermo Soho

- Overview: Tucked away in Palermo Soho, Mine Hotel Boutique offers a blend of comfort and personalized service. The boutique hotel features cozy rooms, a tranquil garden with a pool, and a warm and welcoming atmosphere that reflects the neighborhood's bohemian spirit.

9. Mio Buenos Aires

Location: Av. Quintana 465, Recoleta

- Overview: Mio Buenos Aires, situated in the elegant Recoleta district, is a boutique hotel that exudes contemporary luxury. The hotel's avant-garde design, sleek rooms, and the stylish Mio Restaurant create an ambiance of modern sophistication.

10. 1555 Malabia House Hotel

Location: Malabia 1555, Palermo Soho

- Overview: Housed in a restored mansion in Palermo Soho, 1555 Malabia House Hotel is a boutique retreat with a sense of history. The hotel's individually decorated rooms, charming courtyard, and personalized service make it a quaint and delightful choice.

Buenos Aires, a city known for its vibrant culture and rich history, unfolds its charm through these boutique hotels. Whether nestled in the artistic alleys of Palermo Soho or the trendy streets of Palermo Hollywood, each recommendation invites you to experience the city's spirit in an intimate and unique way. Immerse yourself in the boutique elegance of Buenos Aires, where every stay is a celebration of individuality and style.

Top Bed and Breakfasts in Buenos Aires

For travelers seeking a more intimate and cozy experience in Buenos Aires, the city offers a selection of charming bed and breakfasts. These establishments provide a home away from home, where personalized service, warm hospitality, and a touch of local flavor create a delightful retreat. Here are top recommendations for bed and breakfasts in Buenos Aires, each offering a unique and inviting atmosphere:

1. CasaCalma Hotel

Location: Suipacha 1015, Retiro

- Overview: Tucked away in the Retiro district, CasaCalma Hotel is a serene oasis in the heart of Buenos Aires. This eco-friendly bed and breakfast offer comfortable rooms, a peaceful courtyard, and a commitment to sustainability. Guests can enjoy a relaxing stay within walking distance of key attractions.

2. Anselmo Buenos Aires, Curio Collection by Hilton

Location: Anselmo Aieta 1069, San Telmo

- Overview: In the historic neighborhood of San Telmo, Anselmo Buenos Aires welcomes guests with a blend of elegance and warmth. This bed and breakfast, part of the Curio Collection by Hilton, features stylish rooms, a rooftop terrace with panoramic views, and a central location for exploring the city's cultural treasures.

3. Casa Bevant

Location: Juncal 4461, Palermo Soho

- Overview: Nestled in the trendy Palermo Soho district, Casa Bevant is a cozy bed and breakfast with a homey ambiance. The personalized service, comfortable rooms, and a charming courtyard create a welcoming atmosphere for guests looking to immerse themselves in the bohemian spirit of the neighborhood.

4. Own Madero

Location: Chile 80, Puerto Madero

- Overview: Located in the upscale Puerto Madero district, Own Madero is a boutique bed and breakfast that combines modern comfort with a personalized touch. Guests can enjoy well-appointed rooms, a rooftop pool with city views, and a convenient location near waterfront attractions.

5. Ilum Experience Home

Location: El Salvador 5726, Palermo Hollywood

- Overview: Ilum Experience Home, situated in Palermo Hollywood, offers a boutique bed and breakfast experience. The hotel's contemporary design, spacious rooms, and a tranquil garden with a pool create a relaxing environment for guests to unwind after exploring the vibrant surroundings.

6. Casa Carranza

Location: Carranza 2851, Palermo

- Overview: In the heart of Palermo, Casa Carranza is a charming bed and breakfast housed in a renovated mansion. The boutique accommodation features individually decorated rooms, a cozy courtyard, and a warm and friendly atmosphere that reflects the neighborhood's artistic vibe.

7. Hotel Costa Rica

Location: Costa Rica 4137, Palermo Soho

- Overview: Hotel Costa Rica, located in the heart of Palermo Soho, offers a boutique bed and breakfast experience. With its vibrant decor, comfortable rooms, and a communal terrace, the hotel provides a welcoming retreat in one of Buenos Aires' most lively neighborhoods.

8. Arc Abasto Studios

Location: Yatay 218, Abasto

- Overview: Set in the historic Abasto neighborhood, Arc Abasto Studios is a bed and breakfast that combines modern amenities with a touch of nostalgia. The studios, each with a unique design, provide a comfortable and stylish stay for guests exploring the cultural richness of the area.

9. CasaSur Bellini Hotel

Location: Cabrera 6054, Palermo Hollywood

- Overview: CasaSur Bellini Hotel, located in Palermo Hollywood, offers a boutique bed and breakfast experience with a touch of luxury. The hotel features elegantly appointed rooms, a rooftop terrace with a pool, and a sophisticated ambiance for guests seeking a refined stay.

These top bed and breakfasts in Buenos Aires invite you to experience the city with a personal touch. Whether nestled in the artistic corners of Palermo or the historic streets of San Telmo, each recommendation provides a warm and welcoming haven for travelers looking to immerse themselves in the cultural richness of Buenos Aires. Enjoy the charm and hospitality of these cozy retreats as you create lasting memories in Argentina's vibrant capital.

Top Guesthouses and Inns in Buenos Aires

For travelers seeking a more intimate and locally immersive experience, Buenos Aires offers a range of charming guesthouses and inns. These establishments, often tucked away in historic neighborhoods, provide a welcoming ambiance, personalized service, and a taste of authentic Argentine hospitality. Here are top recommendations for guesthouses and inns in Buenos Aires, each offering a unique and cozy retreat:

1. L'Adresse Hôtel Boutique

Location: Thames 1564, Palermo Soho

- Overview: Nestled in the heart of Palermo Soho, L'Adresse Hôtel Boutique is a quaint guesthouse that combines French-inspired design with Argentine warmth. The individually decorated rooms, a peaceful garden, and the attentive service create a charming escape in one of Buenos Aires' trendiest neighborhoods.

2. La Querencia de Buenos Aires

Location: Carlos Calvo 132, San Telmo

- Overview: In the historic neighborhood of San Telmo, La Querencia de Buenos Aires is a cozy inn that exudes old-world charm. The inn features comfortable rooms, a courtyard with a fountain, and a welcoming atmosphere that reflects the bohemian spirit of the area.

3. Bobo Hotel & Restaurant

Location: Guatemala 4882, Palermo Soho

- Overview: Bobo Hotel & Restaurant, situated in Palermo Soho, is a boutique guesthouse known for its artistic flair. The stylish rooms, a courtyard with a reflecting pool, and the on-site restaurant add to the unique character of this intimate retreat.

4. Viejo Telmo

Location: Chacabuco 861, San Telmo

- Overview: Viejo Telmo, located in San Telmo, is a guesthouse that captures the essence of the neighborhood's historic charm. The inn features cozy rooms, a communal terrace, and a relaxed ambiance, providing guests with a genuine San Telmo experience.

5. La Cayetana

Location: Mexico 1330, San Telmo

- Overview: Set in a restored mansion in San Telmo, La Cayetana is an intimate inn with a touch of elegance. The guesthouse features stylish rooms, a courtyard garden, and a personalized approach to hospitality, inviting guests to experience the historic charm of the neighborhood.

6. Art Factory Palermo

Location: Paraguay 4539, Palermo

- Overview: Art Factory Palermo, located in Palermo, is an artsy guesthouse that doubles as a cultural hub. With its vibrant murals, communal spaces for creativity, and comfortable rooms, the inn provides a unique blend of artistic expression and community spirit.

7. The Glu Boutique Hotel - Palermo Soho

Location: Gurruchaga 1848, Palermo Soho

- Overview: The Glu Boutique Hotel in Palermo Soho is a cozy guesthouse that radiates warmth and hospitality. With its tastefully decorated rooms, a rooftop terrace, and a commitment to personalized service, the inn offers a tranquil respite in the heart of the trendy neighborhood.

8. Art Factory Beer Garden

Location: Paraguay 4539, Palermo

- Overview: Adjacent to Art Factory Palermo, the Beer Garden is a guesthouse extension known for its lively atmosphere. The communal spaces, outdoor seating, and a selection of craft beers create a vibrant and social environment for guests looking to connect with fellow travelers.

9. Five Cool Rooms

Location: Thames 1565, Palermo Hollywood

- Overview: Five Cool Rooms, situated in Palermo Hollywood, is a stylish guesthouse with a modern edge. The contemporary design, comfortable rooms, and a rooftop terrace with a pool add to the chic ambiance of this boutique retreat.

These top guesthouses and inns in Buenos Aires promise a stay that goes beyond accommodation, offering a glimpse into the city's local charm and cultural richness. Whether in the cobblestone streets of San Telmo or the trendy alleys of Palermo, each recommendation invites you to experience Buenos Aires with a personal touch and a warm welcome. Enjoy the authenticity and comfort of these hidden gems as you explore the vibrant spirit of Argentina's capital.

Top Rentals in Buenos Aires

For those seeking the independence and flexibility of a rental accommodation, Buenos Aires offers a variety of options that cater to diverse preferences. Whether you prefer the privacy of an apartment, the charm of a historic home, or the amenities of a modern condo, the city has something to offer. Here are top recommendations for rentals in Buenos Aires, each providing a unique and comfortable retreat:

1. Airbnb

- Overview: Airbnb, a popular platform for short-term rentals, offers a wide array of accommodations in Buenos Aires. From chic apartments in Palermo to historic homes in San Telmo, Airbnb provides options to suit various preferences and budgets.

2. Booking.com Apartments

- Overview: Booking.com, known for its comprehensive booking services, features a range of apartments in Buenos Aires. Travelers can find rentals with diverse amenities, locations, and styles to ensure a comfortable and personalized stay.

3. HomeAway

- Overview: HomeAway, a part of the Vrbo family, specializes in vacation rentals and offers a selection of properties in Buenos Aires. Whether you're looking for a cozy apartment or a spacious house, HomeAway provides options for a home-like experience.

4. Wimdu

- Overview: Wimdu is an online platform that connects travelers with local hosts, offering a variety of rental options in Buenos Aires. From modern apartments to charming studios, Wimdu provides a range of choices for those seeking a personalized stay.

5. Expedia Vacation Rentals

- Overview: Expedia, a renowned travel platform, includes a dedicated section for vacation rentals. Travelers can explore a variety of rental properties in Buenos Aires, from centrally located apartments to cozy homes in residential neighborhoods.

6. ApartmentsBA

- Overview: ApartmentsBA specializes in furnished rental apartments in Buenos Aires, catering to both short-term and long-term stays. The platform offers a curated selection of properties, allowing guests to enjoy the comforts of a home in the heart of the city.

7. Buenos Aires Habitat

- Overview: Buenos Aires Habitat focuses on providing rental apartments in Buenos Aires, with a particular emphasis on personalized service. Whether you're staying in Palermo, Recoleta, or other neighborhoods, Buenos Aires Habitat offers a range of options.

8. Luxury Rentals Buenos Aires

- Overview: For those seeking a touch of luxury, Luxury Rentals Buenos Aires offers high-end rental properties. From stylish penthouses to elegant apartments, this platform caters to travelers looking for a sophisticated and comfortable stay.

9. Rent BA

- Overview: Rent BA specializes in vacation rentals and furnished apartments in Buenos Aires. The platform offers a selection of properties in different neighborhoods, allowing guests to tailor their stay to their preferences.

10. Baires Apartments

- Overview: Baires Apartments provides a variety of rental options in Buenos Aires, including fully equipped apartments for short-term stays. The platform aims to offer a seamless experience for guests looking for a home away from home.

Whether you're planning a short visit or an extended stay in Buenos Aires, these rental platforms provide a diverse range of options to suit every traveler's needs. From budget-friendly apartments to luxurious homes, these rentals offer the convenience and comfort of a personalized retreat, allowing you to experience Buenos Aires at your own pace.

Budget-Friendly Lodgings: Top Hostels in Buenos Aires

For the budget-conscious traveler seeking a sociable and vibrant atmosphere, hostels in Buenos Aires provide an excellent option. These accommodations not only offer affordability but also opportunities to connect with fellow travelers from around the world. Here are top recommendations for hostels in Buenos Aires, each promising a comfortable stay and a chance to immerse yourself in the city's dynamic energy:

1. Milhouse Hostel

Location: Hipólito Yrigoyen 959, San Telmo

- Overview: Milhouse Hostel, located in the historic San Telmo neighborhood, is renowned for its lively atmosphere and social events. With dormitory-style rooms, communal spaces, and a central location, Milhouse is a popular choice for budget travelers looking to make new friends.

2. Hostel Suites Florida

Location: Florida 328, Microcentro

- Overview: Situated in the bustling Microcentro district, Hostel Suites Florida provides budget-friendly accommodation in the heart of Buenos Aires. The hostel offers dormitory and private rooms, and its central location makes it convenient for exploring the city's attractions.

3. Hostel Estoril

Location: Avenida de Mayo 1385, Monserrat

- Overview: Nestled in the historic Monserrat district, Hostel Estoril offers budget-friendly lodging with a focus on comfort. The hostel provides both dormitory and private rooms, and its central location allows easy access to Buenos Aires' cultural and historical sites.

4. Rayuela Hostel

Location: Perú 102, San Telmo

- Overview: Rayuela Hostel, located in the bohemian San Telmo neighborhood, provides a relaxed and friendly atmosphere. With comfortable dorms and communal spaces, the hostel encourages socializing among guests. Its proximity to San Telmo's markets and cafes adds to its appeal.

5. Hostel Suites Obelisco

Location: Corrientes 830, Microcentro

- Overview: Hostel Suites Obelisco, situated in the heart of Microcentro, offers affordable accommodation with easy access to Buenos Aires' main attractions. The hostel provides dormitory and private rooms, making it suitable for both solo travelers and groups.

6. America del Sur Hostel

Location: Chacabuco 718, San Telmo

- Overview: America del Sur Hostel, located in San Telmo, embodies the cultural spirit of Buenos Aires. The hostel features comfortable dorms, communal spaces, and a rooftop terrace with panoramic views of the city, creating a welcoming environment for guests.

7. Hostel Inn Buenos Aires

Location: Avenida de Mayo 1385, Monserrat

- Overview: Hostel Inn Buenos Aires, situated in the historic Monserrat neighborhood, provides budget-friendly lodging with a focus on creating a social atmosphere. The hostel offers dormitory rooms and organizes activities for guests to explore the city together.

8. Pampa Hostel

Location: Bartolomé Mitre 1682, San Nicolás

- Overview: Pampa Hostel, centrally located in San Nicolás, offers budget-friendly accommodation with a friendly and laid-back atmosphere. The hostel provides dormitory-style rooms, and its communal spaces encourage interaction among guests.

9. Hostel Tango Argentina

Location: Estados Unidos 780, San Telmo

- Overview: Set in the heart of San Telmo, Hostel Tango Argentina provides an authentic and budget-friendly experience. The hostel offers dormitory and private rooms, and its proximity to San Telmo's tango clubs and cultural venues adds to its appeal.

These top hostels in Buenos Aires cater to travelers seeking affordability without compromising on comfort and social experiences. Whether you're exploring historic neighborhoods or enjoying the vibrant atmosphere of Palermo, these hostels provide a welcoming base for budget-conscious adventurers looking to make the most of their time in Buenos Aires.

Chapter 5

Outdoor Experiences in Buenos Aires

Buenos Aires, known for its vibrant urban life, also offers a plethora of outdoor adventures for those seeking an adrenaline rush and a connection with nature. From lush parks to water activities, the city provides diverse options to satisfy the outdoor enthusiast in you. Let's dive into the array of outdoor adventures awaiting your exploration in Buenos Aires.

Exploring the Eclectic Parks and Green Spaces

Bosques de Palermo (Palermo Woods)

Overview:

- Bosques de Palermo, the expansive urban park in the heart of Palermo, is a green haven offering a variety of outdoor activities. Whether you prefer jogging along tree-lined paths, rowing on the lake, or picnicking in open spaces, Palermo Woods caters to all.

Activities:

- Jogging and Running Trails: Explore well-maintained trails surrounded by lush greenery.
- Rowing on the Lake: Rent a rowboat and navigate the serene lake at your own pace.
- Cycling: Bring your bike or rent one to pedal through designated cycling lanes.
- Picnics and Relaxation: Enjoy a leisurely day with family and friends in open grassy areas.

Reserva Ecológica Costanera Sur (Costanera Sur Ecological Reserve)

Overview:

- Nestled along the Rio de la Plata, this ecological reserve offers a unique blend of natural landscapes and urban views. It's a haven for birdwatchers, nature lovers, and those seeking a peaceful escape from the bustling city.

Activities:

- Birdwatching: Explore the diverse bird species inhabiting the wetlands and lagoons.
- Walking and Hiking Trails: Follow well-marked trails through marshes, forests, and coastal areas.
- Photography Expeditions: Capture the scenic beauty and urban skyline from designated viewpoints.

Water Adventures along the Rio de la Plata

Sailing and Yachting in the River Plate

Overview:

- The Rio de la Plata, one of the widest rivers in the world, provides an excellent setting for sailing and yachting enthusiasts. Whether you're a seasoned sailor or a beginner, the river's expansive waters offer an exhilarating experience.

Activities:

- Sailing Excursions: Join guided sailing tours for panoramic views of the city skyline.

- Yacht Rentals: Charter a yacht for a private cruise, complete with crew and amenities.
- Sailing Schools: Learn the ropes of sailing with lessons tailored to your skill level.

Kitesurfing and Windsurfing

Overview:

- With its windy conditions, the Rio de la Plata is a hotspot for kitesurfing and windsurfing. Adventure seekers can harness the power of the wind and ride the waves for an adrenaline-pumping experience.

Activities:

- Kitesurfing Lessons: Enroll in lessons to master the art of kitesurfing with certified instructors.
- Windsurfing Rentals: Rent windsurfing equipment and ride the waves at your own pace.
- Proximity to Beaches: Explore beaches like Punta Rasa known for ideal kitesurfing conditions.

Thrilling Urban Adventures

Urban Kayaking in the City Canals

Overview:

- Buenos Aires' intricate network of canals offers a unique urban kayaking experience. Paddle through the city's waterways, exploring its neighborhoods from a different perspective.

Activities:

- Guided Kayak Tours: Join guided tours to navigate the canals and learn about the city's history.
- Kayak Rentals: Rent a kayak and embark on a self-guided adventure through the urban waterways.
- Night Kayaking: Experience the city lights and reflections on the water with evening kayak excursions.

Rock Climbing in Natural and Urban Settings

Overview:

- For those seeking vertical challenges, Buenos Aires presents both natural and urban rock climbing options. Climb rugged cliffs or tackle climbing walls within the city for an exhilarating experience.

Activities:

- Outdoor Climbing Excursions: Join guided climbing tours to natural rock formations outside the city.
- Indoor Climbing Gyms: Explore indoor climbing gyms offering various levels of difficulty.
- Training Courses: Enroll in rock climbing courses suitable for beginners and advanced climbers.

Biking Adventures Through the City Streets

Urban Bike Tours

Overview:

- Buenos Aires' flat terrain and bike-friendly streets make it an ideal city for cycling enthusiasts. Join urban bike tours to explore the city's neighborhoods, historical sites, and vibrant street art.

Activities:

- Guided Bike Tours: Discover iconic landmarks and hidden gems with knowledgeable guides.
- Bike Rentals: Explore the city independently by renting a bike from various rental services.
- Cycling Events: Participate in cycling events and group rides for a social biking experience.

Mountain Biking in Surrounding Natural Reserves

Overview:

- Escape the urban hustle and explore the rugged terrains surrounding Buenos Aires on a mountain bike. Natural reserves and trails offer varying levels of difficulty for mountain biking enthusiasts.

Activities:

- Mountain Biking Trails: Navigate through scenic trails in natural reserves and green spaces.
- Organized Mountain Biking Events: Participate in organized events for a challenging and social experience.
- Bike Rentals and Tours: Rent mountain bikes and join guided tours tailored to different skill levels.

Aerial Adventures: Paragliding and Skydiving

Paragliding Over the Suburbs and Coastal Areas

Overview:

- Experience the thrill of soaring through the skies with paragliding adventures in the suburbs and coastal regions surrounding Buenos Aires. Enjoy panoramic views as you glide gracefully above the landscapes.

Activities:

- Tandem Paragliding: Opt for tandem paragliding experiences with certified instructors.
- Scenic Flights: Soar over scenic landscapes, including coastal areas and suburbs.
- Training Courses: Enroll in paragliding courses for those looking to master the sport.

Skydiving Over the Countryside

Overview:

- For the ultimate adrenaline rush, embark on a skydiving adventure over the picturesque countryside surrounding Buenos Aires. Feel the exhilaration of freefall and enjoy breathtaking views as you descend.

Activities:

- Tandem Skydiving: Experience the thrill of skydiving with tandem jumps accompanied by instructors.
- Accelerated Freefall Courses: Enroll in courses for those seeking to become certified skydivers.
- Safety Briefings: Prioritize safety with comprehensive briefings and equipment checks.

Nature Retreats: Hiking and Wildlife Exploration

Hiking in the Sierras de la Ventana

Overview:

- Escape the urban environment and venture into the Sierras de la Ventana, a mountain range near Buenos Aires, for hiking adventures. Explore scenic trails, picturesque viewpoints, and lush landscapes.

Activities:

- Guided Hiking Tours: Join guided tours for insights into the region's flora, fauna, and geological features.
- Mountain Summit Treks: Challenge yourself with hikes leading to the summits for panoramic views.
- Camping Expeditions: Extend your outdoor experience with camping expeditions in the mountain range.

Wildlife Safari in Reserva Otamendi

Overview:

- For nature enthusiasts, Reserva Otamendi offers a unique wildlife safari experience near Buenos Aires. Explore the reserve's diverse ecosystems and encounter native species in their natural habitats.

Activities:

- Safari Tours: Join safari tours led by knowledgeable guides for wildlife observation.
- Birdwatching: Spot a variety of bird species that inhabit the reserve's wetlands and forests.
- Photography Safaris: Capture stunning wildlife moments in their natural settings.

Safety Considerations and Tips for Outdoor Adventures

While engaging in outdoor adventures in Buenos Aires, prioritizing safety is paramount. Follow these general safety considerations and tips to ensure a secure and enjoyable experience:

1. General Safety Tips

- Equipment Check: Ensure all adventure equipment is in good condition before use.
- Weather Awareness: Check weather forecasts and avoid outdoor activities during adverse conditions.
- Emergency Contacts: Carry emergency contact information and know the location of nearby medical facilities.

2. Water Safety Tips

- Life Jackets: Use appropriate safety gear, such as life jackets, during water activities.
- Swimming Skills: Ensure adequate swimming skills before participating in water adventures.
- Supervised Activities: Opt for guided water activities with trained instructors.

3. Heights and Aerial Adventures Safety Tips

- Certified Instructors: Choose activities with certified instructors and reputable providers.
- Equipment Inspection: Verify the condition of parachutes, harnesses, and safety gear before skydiving.

- Health Check: Ensure participants meet health requirements for aerial activities.

4. Urban Adventures Safety Tips

- Traffic Awareness: Exercise caution when cycling or participating in urban adventures near traffic.
- Helmet Usage: Always wear helmets during biking adventures for head protection.
- Follow Rules: Adhere to traffic rules and guidelines for safe urban adventures.

Embark on an exhilarating journey of outdoor adventures in Buenos Aires, where the city's vibrant energy extends beyond its urban boundaries. Whether you're soaring through the skies, navigating waterways, or trekking in natural reserves, Buenos Aires offers a diverse range of outdoor experiences for every adventurer.

Chapter 6

Savoring the Culinary Delights

Argentine Traditional Delicacies

Argentina's rich culinary tapestry is woven with a diverse array of traditional delicacies, each reflecting the country's cultural influences and regional variations. From sizzling meats prepared in the iconic asado to delectable pastries and sweets that satisfy the sweet tooth, Argentine cuisine is a celebration of flavor and tradition. Let's embark on a comprehensive exploration of some of the most beloved traditional delicacies that define the gastronomic landscape of Argentina:

1. Asado: The Epitome of Argentine Culinary Culture

- At the heart of Argentine gastronomy lies the revered tradition of asado, a quintessential barbecue experience. Asado is not merely a meal; it's a social event, a time-honored ritual where family and friends gather to share in the pleasure of grilled meats. Various cuts, including ribs, flank steak, and sausages, are carefully seasoned and slow-cooked over an open flame or parrilla. The result is succulent, flavorful meat, often enjoyed with chimichurri sauce—a zesty blend of parsley, garlic, vinegar, and spices.

2. Empanadas: Handheld Parcels of Flavor

- Empanadas are savory turnovers that encapsulate the diverse flavors of Argentina. These hand-held delights feature a delicate pastry shell, filled with a range of savory ingredients. Common fillings include minced beef, onions, olives, hard-boiled eggs, and spices, creating a harmonious blend of textures and tastes. Empanadas are enjoyed as a quick snack, appetizer, or integral part of festive occasions.

3. Matambre a la Pizza: A Pizza-Style Twist on Flank Steak

- Matambre, a cut of beef from the flank or chest, takes on a unique Argentine flair with Matambre a la Pizza. This dish transforms the meat into a pizza-style creation. The flank steak is seasoned and cooked "pizza style," adorned with a flavorful mixture of herbs, tomatoes, and cheese. The result is a mouthwatering fusion of the traditional Argentine asado with the beloved elements of a classic pizza.

4. Locro: Hearty Stew Celebrating Indigenous Roots

- Locro is a hearty and aromatic stew that pays homage to Argentina's indigenous heritage. The dish features hominy corn, meats such as beef, pork, and chorizo, vegetables, and spices. Locro is often associated with patriotic celebrations, especially during national holidays, and its robust flavors offer a comforting and satisfying dining experience.

5. Humita en Chala: Steamed Corn Pudding Wrapped in Corn Husks

- Humita en Chala is a traditional dish that showcases the abundance of corn in Argentine cuisine. Grated corn is mixed with sautéed onions, cheese, and spices, wrapped in corn husks, and steamed to perfection. The result is a flavorful and aromatic corn pudding, a testament to the culinary ingenuity of Argentina's diverse regions.

6. Provoleta: Grilled Cheese Excellence

- Provoleta is a simple yet irresistible appetizer that highlights Argentina's love affair with cheese. A wheel of provolone cheese is seasoned with oregano and chili flakes, then grilled until melted and bubbly. Served hot and gooey, provoleta is a popular starter at asado gatherings, enticing diners with its cheesy goodness.

7. Milanesa: Breaded and Fried Comfort Food

- Inspired by Italian culinary influences, Milanesa is a beloved Argentine comfort food. Thinly sliced meat, typically beef or chicken, is breaded and fried until golden brown. Milanesa is often served with mashed potatoes, a simple salad, or as a sandwich known as milanesa a la napolitana, layered with ham, marinara sauce, and melted cheese.

8. Dulce de Leche: Sweet Caramel Elixir

- Dulce de leche is a sweet and velvety caramel spread that occupies a special place in Argentine desserts. Made from condensed milk, this rich delicacy is used to fill pastries, top pancakes, and sweeten various treats. Whether enjoyed on toast or as a decadent addition to desserts, dulce de leche is a sweet symphony that defines Argentine sweetness.

9. Choripán: Street Food Extravaganza

- Choripán exemplifies the art of simplicity in Argentine street food. A portmanteau of "chorizo" (sausage) and "pan" (bread), choripán is a grilled chorizo sausage sandwiched in a crusty roll. The chorizo is often seasoned with chimichurri, adding an extra layer of flavor to this popular street food delight.

10. Alfajores: Sweet Sandwich Cookies with Dulce de Leche

- Alfajores are sweet treats that epitomize Argentine confectionery. These delicate sandwich cookies consist of two buttery biscuits sandwiching a generous layer of dulce de leche. Some variations are coated in chocolate or powdered sugar, adding an extra layer of indulgence to these beloved sweets.

11. Puchero: A Hearty Pot of Culinary History

- Puchero is a robust and wholesome stew that reflects Argentina's culinary history. The dish combines a variety of meats, vegetables, and legumes, creating a nourishing pot of goodness. Puchero is often associated with familial warmth, and its rich flavors are a testament to the agricultural abundance that defines Argentine cuisine.

12. Humita: Steamed Corn Tamale

- Humita is a traditional Argentine tamale, featuring a filling of grated corn mixed with sautéed onions, cheese, **and** spices. The mixture is encased in corn husks and steamed to perfection. The result is a flavorful and comforting dish that pays homage to the culinary heritage of Argentina's indigenous communities.

13. Medialunas: Crescent-Shaped Morning Delights

- Medialunas are flaky, crescent-shaped pastries that are a staple of Argentine breakfasts and meriendas (afternoon snacks). These delicate pastries come in two varieties: medialunas de manteca, made with butter, and medialunas de grasa, made with lard. Enjoyed with a cup of coffee or mate, medialunas are a delightful way to start or punctuate the day.

14. Chocotorta: No-Bake Chocolate Cookie Cake

- Chocotorta is a popular no-bake dessert that showcases the simplicity of Argentine home baking. The dessert layers chocolate cookies with a filling made from cream cheese and dulce de leche. Chilled to perfection, Chocotorta is a crowd-pleaser at family gatherings and celebrations.

15. Argentine Wine: A Toast to Vineyard Excellence

- Argentina's wine culture is deeply intertwined with its culinary traditions. Malbec, a robust red wine, is Argentina's flagship varietal and pairs impeccably with the country's bold flavors. The country's diverse wine regions, including Mendoza and Salta, contribute to the production of high-quality wines that enhance the dining experience and reflect Argentina's status as a global wine powerhouse.

From the sizzle of asado on the grill to the sweet indulgence of alfajores, Argentine traditional delicacies invite you to savor the flavors of a nation deeply connected to its culinary roots. Each dish tells a story, a narrative of history, geography, and cultural heritage, making the culinary journey through Argentina a sensory exploration of traditions passed down through generations.

Fine Dining in Buenos Aires

Buenos Aires, a city steeped in cultural richness, offers a fine dining scene that is as diverse as it is sophisticated. From traditional Argentine flavors to avant-garde culinary creations, the city's top-tier restaurants deliver an exquisite gastronomic experience. Here, we explore some of the finest establishments in Buenos Aires, where culinary artistry and luxurious settings converge to create a memorable journey for the discerning palate.

1. Tegui: Modern Argentine Culinary Mastery

Overview: Tegui, nestled in the chic Palermo neighborhood, stands as a beacon of modern Argentine cuisine. Chef Germán Martitegui, a culinary maestro, curates a tasting menu that celebrates the essence of local ingredients with a contemporary twist. The Michelin-starred restaurant's minimalist décor and intimate ambiance provide the perfect canvas for a culinary masterpiece.

- Signature Dishes: Patagonian lamb with Andean potatoes, squid ink risotto with Argentine shrimp, and dulce de leche mousse with passion fruit.

2. Don Julio: Timeless Argentine Steakhouse Elegance

Overview: Don Julio, located in the Palermo Soho neighborhood, is an iconic parrilla (grill) that embodies the essence of traditional Argentine steakhouses. The warm, rustic atmosphere and impeccable service complement the star of the show – perfectly grilled Argentine steaks. The extensive wine selection ensures a delightful pairing for a classic and satisfying meal.

- Signature Dishes: Bife de chorizo (sirloin steak), empanadas, and provoleta (melted provolone cheese).

3. El Preferido de Palermo: Nostalgic Elegance with a Culinary Flair

Overview: El Preferido de Palermo seamlessly combines timeless elegance with a touch of nostalgia. Located in Palermo Hollywood, this historic restaurant serves classic Argentine dishes with a focus on quality ingredients and meticulous preparation. The vintage ambiance, characterized by wooden accents and vintage photos, enhances the overall dining experience.

- Signature Dishes: Milanesa a la Napolitana, locro (Argentine stew), and flan with dulce de leche.

Buenos Aires' fine dining establishments offer a symphony of flavors, blending the rich culinary traditions of Argentina with contemporary culinary innovation. Whether indulging in the modern Argentine creations at Tegui or savoring the timeless elegance of a steakhouse experience at Don Julio, each of these top recommendations promises an unforgettable culinary journey in the heart of this vibrant city.

Casual Eateries in Buenos Aires

While Buenos Aires is known for its sophisticated fine dining scene, the city also boasts a vibrant array of casual eateries where locals and visitors alike can savor delicious meals in a laid-back atmosphere. From traditional parrillas to trendy cafes, here are some top recommendations for casual dining experiences that capture the essence of Buenos Aires' culinary charm.

1. La Cabrera: Parrilla Passion with a Cozy Ambiance

La Cabrera, located in Palermo, is a renowned parrilla that offers a quintessential Argentine dining experience in a relaxed setting. Known for its mouthwatering steaks and generous portions, La Cabrera is a favorite among locals. The cozy ambiance, adorned with rustic decor and friendly staff, makes it an ideal spot for a casual and hearty meal.

- Must-Try Dishes: Bife de chorizo (sirloin steak), provoleta (melted provolone cheese), and empanadas.

2. El Preferido de Palermo: Classic Comfort in Palermo Hollywood

El Preferido de Palermo seamlessly combines timeless elegance with a casual atmosphere. Located in Palermo Hollywood, this eatery serves classic Argentine comfort food in a charming setting. Wooden accents and vintage photos create a cozy ambiance, making it a delightful spot for a laid-back lunch or dinner.

- Must-Try Dishes: Locro (Argentine stew), milanesa a la Napolitana, and flan with dulce de leche.

3. Las Cabras: Lively Atmosphere with Outdoor Seating

Las Cabras, situated in Palermo, is a lively parrilla known for its vibrant atmosphere and delicious grilled meats. The restaurant features outdoor seating, creating a relaxed environment to enjoy the flavors of Argentine barbecue. The extensive menu and friendly service make Las Cabras a popular choice for those seeking a casual and authentic dining experience.

- Must-Try Dishes: Asado (barbecue), choripán (sausage sandwich), and grilled vegetables.

4. Don Ernesto: Homestyle Comfort in San Telmo

Don Ernesto, nestled in the historic San Telmo neighborhood, exudes homestyle comfort in a casual setting. This eatery focuses on traditional Argentine dishes prepared with love and attention to detail. The welcoming atmosphere and straightforward menu make it a go-to spot for those craving authentic flavors without the fuss.

- Must-Try Dishes: Matambre a la pizza (flank steak with pizza toppings), pastel de papa (potato pie), and alfajores for dessert.

5. Pain et Vin: Charming Café with European Flair

Pain et Vin, located in Recoleta, is a charming café that brings a touch of European flair to Buenos Aires. With its cozy interior and sidewalk seating, it's an ideal spot for a leisurely brunch or coffee break. The menu features a selection of sandwiches, pastries, and artisanal bread, making it a delightful choice for a casual and delightful meal.

- Must-Try Items: Croque monsieur, quiche, and a selection of freshly baked bread.

6. Oui Oui: Trendy Café in Palermo Soho

Oui Oui, situated in the trendy Palermo Soho neighborhood, is a trendy café that combines a relaxed atmosphere with a menu of delectable dishes. Known for its brunch offerings and French-inspired pastries, Oui Oui is a favorite among locals seeking a casual and stylish setting to enjoy a leisurely meal.

- Must-Try Items: Eggs Benedict, French toast, and a variety of artisanal pastries.

7. La Cocina: Local Flavors in San Telmo Market

La Cocina, located within the historic San Telmo Market, is a casual eatery that celebrates local flavors and market-fresh ingredients. With its communal tables and bustling atmosphere, it provides an authentic experience of Argentine cuisine. Visitors can enjoy a diverse range of dishes, from empanadas to traditional stews.

- Must-Try Dishes: Empanadas, locro, and chorizo sandwiches.

8. Hierbabuena: Healthy Fare in Palermo Hollywood

Hierbabuena, nestled in Palermo Hollywood, offers a refreshing take on casual dining with its focus on healthy and flavorful dishes. The menu features a variety of salads, wraps, and smoothies, making it a popular choice for those seeking a lighter and nutritious meal in a laid-back setting.

- Must-Try Items: Quinoa salad, avocado toast, and fresh fruit smoothies.

9. Mishiguene: Jewish-Inspired Delights in Palermo

Mishiguene, located in Palermo, adds a unique twist to casual dining with its Jewish-inspired menu. The cozy and eclectic ambiance sets the stage for a culinary journey that blends traditional Argentine flavors with Jewish culinary heritage. It's an ideal spot for those looking to explore inventive and comforting dishes in a relaxed atmosphere.

- Must-Try Dishes: Matzo ball soup, pastrami sandwich, and babka for dessert.

10. La Mezzetta: Pizza Paradise in Almagro

La Mezzetta, situated in the Almagro neighborhood, is a beloved pizzeria that captures the essence of casual dining in Buenos Aires. With its no-frills setting and a focus on classic pizza recipes, it has become a go-to spot for locals craving delicious and straightforward comfort food.

- Must-Try Pizzas: Margherita, fugazzeta (onion and cheese), and a variety of toppings to suit your taste.

Buenos Aires' casual eateries offer a diverse array of culinary experiences, from traditional parrillas to trendy cafes and eclectic spots that blend flavors from different culinary traditions. Whether you're savoring a juicy steak at La Cabrera or enjoying a leisurely brunch at Oui Oui, these top recommendations promise a delightful and relaxed dining experience in the heart of this vibrant city.

Dining Etiquette and Tips in Buenos Aires

Buenos Aires, with its rich cultural heritage and diverse culinary scene, has its own set of dining customs and etiquette. Understanding and embracing these traditions can enhance your dining experience and allow you to immerse yourself fully in the local culture. Here are some essential dining etiquette and tips to keep in mind when enjoying meals in Buenos Aires:

1. Embrace the Late Dining Culture:

In Buenos Aires, dinner is typically enjoyed later than in many other parts of the world. It's common for locals to start dining around 8:00 PM or even later. Restaurants and cafes come to life in the evening, creating a vibrant atmosphere that continues well into the night. Embrace the leisurely pace and enjoy the lively ambiance.

2. Learn the Art of Mate Sharing:

Mate, a traditional Argentine herbal tea, is often shared among friends and family. If someone offers you a mate, it's a gesture of hospitality and friendship. When handed the mate, drink the entire portion and return the empty mate to the person who poured it for you. Refusing a mate is considered impolite, so be open to participating in this social ritual.

3. Master the Art of Parrilla Ordering:

When dining at a parrilla (steakhouse), understanding how to order your steak is crucial. Beef cuts are a matter of personal preference, but some popular choices include bife de chorizo (sirloin), entraña (skirt steak), and vacío (flank). Steaks are often served rare or medium-rare unless you specify otherwise. Don't forget to pair your steak with chimichurri, a flavorful sauce made with herbs, garlic, and vinegar.

4. Understand the Cover Charge Concept:

It's common for restaurants in Buenos Aires to have a cover charge, known as "cubierto." This charge covers the cost of bread, table service, and sometimes includes a small appetizer. It's usually a fixed amount per person, so be prepared for this additional fee when reviewing the menu.

5. Tipping Etiquette:

Tipping is customary in Buenos Aires, and it's customary to leave around 10% to 15% of the total bill as a tip. Some restaurants may include a service charge (servicio) on the bill, so check before adding an additional tip. Tipping is also appreciated in cafes and bars, and rounding up the bill is a common practice.

6. Navigating Wine Culture:

Argentina is renowned for its exceptional wines, and exploring the local wine culture is a must. When ordering wine, you can ask the waiter or sommelier for recommendations based on your preferences. Malbec is the flagship red wine, but there are many other excellent varietals to discover. It's acceptable to taste the wine before approving, and it's appreciated if you toast with your dining companions before taking the first sip.

7. Respect Local Dining Customs:

Argentines value their time spent at the table, emphasizing the social aspect of dining. Engage in conversation, enjoy the company of your fellow diners, and savor the flavors of each dish. Rushing through a meal is not in line with local customs, so take your time and relish the dining experience.

8. Cash is King:

While credit cards are widely accepted, it's advisable to carry some cash, especially in smaller establishments or street markets. Cash can also be handy for leaving tips, as not all places provide an option to add it to the credit card payment.

9. Politeness Goes a Long Way:

Politeness and courtesy are highly valued in Argentine culture. Greet the staff with a friendly "Hola" (hello) and express gratitude with a "Gracias" (thank you). Basic Spanish phrases can go a long way in making your dining experience more enjoyable.

10. Reservations Recommended:

In popular restaurants, especially on weekends, making a reservation is advisable. Buenos Aires has a thriving culinary scene, and popular establishments can fill up quickly. Reserving a table ensures you won't miss out on a memorable dining experience.

By embracing these dining etiquette tips, you'll not only enjoy the delectable flavors of Buenos Aires but also immerse yourself in the warmth and hospitality of Argentine culture. Buenos provechos! (Enjoy your meal!)

Chapter 7

Shopping Escapades

A Culinary Adventure through Local Markets

Buenos Aires, a city steeped in cultural richness, offers a plethora of local markets that provide a sensory feast for both locals and visitors. These markets showcase Argentina's diverse culinary landscape, from traditional meats and mate to artisanal crafts. Let's dive into some of the top local markets and their recommendations for an authentic Buenos Aires experience:

1. Feria de Mataderos: A Cultural Extravaganza

Location: Mataderos neighborhood

Highlights:

- Artisan Crafts: Explore handmade crafts and traditional Argentine artwork, offering a glimpse into the country's folk traditions.
- Live Performances: Enjoy live folk music and traditional dance performances, immersing yourself in Argentina's rich cultural heritage.
- Gastronomic Delights: Sample regional dishes such as empanadas, locro (a hearty stew), and asado (barbecue).

2. San Telmo Market: Historic and Artistic

Location: San Telmo neighborhood

Highlights:

- Antique Finds: Stroll through the market's antique section, where you can discover vintage treasures, from furniture to trinkets.
- Local Artisans: Engage with local artisans selling handmade jewelry, textiles, and unique crafts.
- Street Performers: Encounter street performers adding to the bohemian atmosphere of the market.
- Foodie Paradise: Savor Argentine street food, including choripán (sausage sandwich) and freshly squeezed fruit juices.

3. Mercado de Abasto: Gastronomic Haven

Location: Abasto neighborhood

Highlights:

- Fresh Produce: Explore the market's fruit and vegetable stalls, offering a colorful array of locally sourced produce.
- Gourmet Delights: Discover gourmet food shops, including cheese and wine stores, where you can indulge in high-quality Argentine delicacies.
- Tango Connection: Visit the Carlos Gardel Museum within the market, celebrating the iconic tango singer.

4. Mercado de San Telmo: Traditional and Lively

Location: San Telmo neighborhood

Highlights:

- Meat Market: Immerse yourself in the vibrant atmosphere of the meat market, where local butchers showcase Argentina's renowned beef cuts.

- Craft Beers: Sample craft beers at the market's microbreweries, offering a taste of the burgeoning beer scene in Buenos Aires.
- Live Music: Enjoy live music performances, adding to the lively ambiance of this traditional market.

5. Feria de Mataderos: A Gaucho Experience

Location: Mataderos neighborhood

Highlights:

- Gaucho Traditions: Witness traditional gaucho (Argentine cowboy) skills, including horsemanship and rodeo demonstrations.
- Regional Cuisine: Indulge in regional delicacies such as empanadas salteñas, a variation of the classic empanada from Salta province.
- Handicrafts: Browse through stalls selling handmade leather goods, textiles, and indigenous crafts.

6. Feria de San Pedro Telmo: Vintage Finds and More

Location: San Telmo neighborhood

Highlights:

- Vintage Treasures: Explore the market's antique section, where you can find vintage clothing, books, and unique collectibles.
- Live Music and Dance: Experience impromptu tango and live music performances that contribute to the market's lively atmosphere.

- Diverse Cuisine: Choose from a variety of international and local food stalls, offering everything from Argentine barbecue to international street food.

7. Mercado de Pulgas: Antique Treasure Hunt

Location: Palermo Hollywood neighborhood

Highlights:

- Antique Market: Delve into the treasure trove of antique furniture, vintage clothing, and eclectic finds in this market.
- Artisan Crafts: Discover unique handmade crafts and artisanal products that make for distinctive souvenirs.
- Eclectic Atmosphere: Enjoy the quirky and eclectic atmosphere of Palermo Hollywood, with trendy cafes and boutiques surrounding the market.

9. Mercado de San Nicolás: Historic Splendor

Location: Microcentro neighborhood

Highlights:

- Architectural Beauty: Admire the historic building housing the market, showcasing architectural elegance from the early 20th century.
- Culinary Delights: Indulge in traditional Argentine dishes at the market's diverse food stalls, offering a culinary journey through local flavors.

10. Mercado de Belgrano: Hidden Gem

Location: Belgrano neighborhood

Highlights:

- Local Produce: Wander through stalls offering fresh fruits, vegetables, and regional products.
- Cafés and Bakeries: Enjoy a leisurely coffee or indulge in delicious pastries at the market's cozy cafes and bakeries.
- Artisanal Goods: Discover handmade goods and artisanal products, providing a taste of the neighborhood's local charm.

Buenos Aires' local markets are not just places to shop for fresh produce or unique crafts; they are vibrant hubs that encapsulate the spirit of the city. From the historic charm of San Telmo to the cultural extravaganza in Mataderos, each market offers a unique experience that allows you to immerse yourself in Buenos Aires' culinary and cultural richness. Whether you're on the hunt for vintage treasures, savoring traditional Argentine dishes, or enjoying live performances, these markets beckon you to explore the heart and soul of Buenos Aires.

High-End and Contemporary Shopping

Buenos Aires, a city that seamlessly fuses tradition with contemporary flair, boasts a vibrant scene for high-end and modern shopping. From cutting-edge fashion boutiques to sleek concept stores, the Argentine capital invites discerning shoppers into a world where innovation meets luxury. Here are some top recommendations for indulging in high-end and modern shopping experiences in Buenos Aires:

1. Alcorta Shopping: The Epitome of Modern Luxury

Alcorta Shopping, located in the upscale Palermo district, stands as a testament to modern luxury. This shopping destination features a curated selection of high-end international brands, offering a diverse range of fashion, accessories, and lifestyle products. With its contemporary architecture and sophisticated ambiance, Alcorta Shopping sets the stage for a premium shopping experience.

- Top Recommendations: Armani Exchange for modern elegance; Zara Home for chic home decor.

2. Distrito Arcos: Urban Chic in Las Cañitas

Distrito Arcos, nestled in the trendy Las Cañitas neighborhood, is a modern shopping center that captures the essence of urban chic. The open-air complex hosts a mix of local and international brands, emphasizing contemporary fashion and lifestyle. Distrito Arcos provides a stylish setting for those seeking cutting-edge designs and a relaxed shopping atmosphere.

- Top Recommendations: Nike Store for sporty sophistication; Material for avant-garde jewelry.

3. Patio Bullrich: Timeless Elegance with a Modern Twist

Patio Bullrich, a historic shopping center, seamlessly combines timeless elegance with modern sophistication. Located in the heart of the city, this upscale mall features a carefully curated selection of high-end brands, including both iconic names and emerging designers. From fashion to technology, Patio Bullrich offers a modern shopping experience within a classic architectural setting.

- Top Recommendations: Apple Store for cutting-edge technology; Carolina Herrera for timeless fashion.

4. Paseo Alcorta: Contemporary Fashion Hub

Paseo Alcorta, situated in the Palermo district, is a contemporary shopping center that caters to those with a penchant for modern fashion. The mall boasts a diverse array of high-end stores, blending international brands with local designers. Paseo Alcorta provides a dynamic space where fashion-forward trends meet a sophisticated shopping environment.

- Top Recommendations: H&M for fast-fashion trends; Prüne for modern Argentine accessories.

5. Galerías Pacífico: Artistic Fusion of Past and Present

Galerías Pacífico, located on Florida Street, is not just a shopping mall; it's a canvas where modern luxury intertwines with artistic heritage. This historic building, adorned with murals and frescoes, houses an array of high-end and contemporary brands. Galerías Pacífico offers a unique blend of culture and commerce, creating a shopping experience that transcends time.

- Top Recommendations: Tommy Hilfiger for classic American style; Swarovski for modern crystal creations.

6. Soho Mall: Trendsetting Styles in Palermo Soho

Soho Mall, situated in the trendy Palermo Soho neighborhood, is a fashion-forward destination that celebrates modern styles. This concept shopping center hosts a mix of international and local designers, providing a platform for emerging trends and contemporary aesthetics. Soho Mall invites shoppers to explore the cutting edge of fashion in a vibrant and dynamic setting.

- Top Recommendations: Adidas Originals for streetwear chic; Rapsodia for bohemian-inspired fashion.

7. Abasto Shopping: Family-Friendly Modernity

Abasto Shopping, located in the Abasto neighborhood, offers a modern and family-friendly shopping experience. This expansive mall features a blend of high-end and mid-range stores, catering to a diverse range of tastes. With its contemporary design and entertainment options, Abasto Shopping is a modern hub for both fashion and leisure.

- Top Recommendations: Levi's Store for casual cool; Falabella for modern home goods.

8. Punta Carretas Shopping: Contemporary Luxury in Recoleta

Punta Carretas Shopping, situated in the Recoleta neighborhood, is a modern shopping center that exudes luxury and contemporary style. With its sleek design and diverse selection of high-end brands, the mall caters to a sophisticated clientele. Punta Carretas Shopping provides an upscale environment for those seeking the latest trends and modern luxuries.

- Top Recommendations: Calvin Klein for minimalist sophistication; La Martina for premium polo-inspired fashion.

9. Unicenter: Modernity in the Northern Suburbs

Unicenter, located in the northern suburbs, is one of the largest shopping centers in Buenos Aires, offering a modern retail experience outside the city center. With its expansive layout and diverse mix of stores, Unicenter is a hub for contemporary fashion, technology, and lifestyle products.

- Top Recommendations: Sony Store for cutting-edge electronics; MAC Cosmetics for modern beauty.

10. Galería Bond Street: Alternative Modernity

Galería Bond Street, nestled in the heart of the city, caters to those with an alternative and modern taste. This unique shopping destination is known for its diverse collection of stores specializing in music, fashion, and urban culture. Galería Bond Street is a haven for those seeking a break from mainstream shopping.

- Top Recommendations: El Burgués for alternative fashion; Rockland for music memorabilia.

Indulging in high-end and modern shopping in Buenos Aires is a journey into the city's contemporary soul. From the chic boutiques of Palermo to the historic elegance of Patio Bullrich, each destination invites you to explore the latest trends and cutting-edge designs in a city that seamlessly blends tradition with modernity.

Discovering Buenos Aires through Souvenirs

Buenos Aires, a city that pulsates with energy and cultural richness, offers an array of unique souvenirs that encapsulate its vibrant spirit. Whether you're strolling through historic markets, exploring eclectic boutiques, or immersing yourself in traditional crafts, Buenos Aires has something special for every traveler. Here's a guide to the distinctive souvenirs that capture the essence of this captivating city:

1. Mate Sets: Sipping Tradition

Mate, a traditional Argentine herbal tea, is more than a beverage; it's a cultural symbol. Bring home a mate set, typically consisting of a carved gourd (mate) and a metal straw (bombilla), to experience this beloved ritual. Look for artisanal mate sets with intricate carvings or opt for modern designs that blend tradition with contemporary flair.

- Where to Find: San Telmo Market, Feria de Mataderos, and specialty boutiques.

2. Leather Goods: Argentine Elegance

Argentina is renowned for its high-quality leather, making leather goods a quintessential Buenos Aires souvenir. From stylish wallets and belts to handcrafted bags and jackets, the options are diverse. Look for items made from Argentine cowhide, and consider personalized pieces for a truly unique keepsake.

- Where to Find: Avenida Alvear boutiques, San Telmo leather shops, and Paseo Alcorta.

3. Tango Memorabilia: Dance to Remember

Tango, the passionate dance that originated in Buenos Aires, is an integral part of the city's identity. Bring home a piece of tango culture with souvenirs like tango-themed artwork, music CDs, or even a pair of authentic tango shoes. These items capture the rhythm and romance of Buenos Aires' iconic dance.

- Where to Find: San Telmo Market, tango show venues, and specialized dance stores.

4. Handwoven Textiles: Crafted Elegance

Argentina's rich textile tradition is reflected in its beautifully crafted ponchos, scarves, and blankets. Look for textiles made from natural fibers like alpaca or llama wool, showcasing traditional patterns and vibrant colors. These handwoven pieces not only keep you warm but also tell a story of Argentine craftsmanship.

- Where to Find: Feria de Mataderos, artisan markets, and boutique stores.

5. Quirky Street Art: Urban Expressions

Buenos Aires is celebrated for its vibrant street art scene, and you can bring a piece of this urban expression home. Look for items adorned with reproductions of famous street art murals, such as posters, postcards, or even wearable art like T-shirts. It's a unique way to carry a bit of Buenos Aires' creative spirit with you.

- Where to Find: Palermo neighborhoods, especially in Palermo Soho and Palermo Hollywood.

6. Argentine Wine: A Toast to Memories

Argentina is renowned for its exceptional wines, particularly the robust Malbec. Bring home a bottle or two of Argentine wine as a flavorful reminder of your time in Buenos Aires. Consider visiting a local winery or wine shop to discover unique varietals and vintages.

- Where to Find: Wine shops in Palermo, specialty wine boutiques, and duty-free stores.

7. Evita Perón Memorabilia: Iconic Legacy

Evita Perón, the iconic First Lady of Argentina, holds a significant place in the nation's history. Souvenirs featuring her image, quotes, or iconic moments are a poignant way to remember her legacy. Look for items like postcards, posters, or even small sculptures.

- Where to Find: Evita Museum gift shop, San Telmo antique stores, and cultural centers.

8. Traditional Argentine Jewelry: Silver Elegance

Argentina is renowned for its silver craftsmanship, and traditional Argentine jewelry makes for exquisite souvenirs. From intricately designed rings and bracelets to earrings inspired by indigenous motifs, these pieces showcase the country's rich cultural heritage.

- Where to Find: Avenida Alvear jewelry boutiques, San Telmo artisan markets, and upscale jewelry stores.

9. Yerba Mate Accessories: Sip in Style

Enhance your mate-drinking experience with stylish yerba mate accessories. Look for artisanal mate cups, bombillas (metal straws), and even yerba mate blends that come in decorative packaging. These accessories add a touch of Argentine tradition to your daily ritual.

- Where to Find: San Telmo Market, specialty mate stores, and artisan fairs.

10. Argentine Artisanal Chocolates: Sweet Indulgences

Argentina is known for its delectable chocolates, often made from high-quality cocoa beans. Bring home a box of artisanal chocolates featuring unique flavors such as dulce de leche, malbec-infused, or yerba mate-infused. These sweet treats make for delightful gifts.

- Where to Find: Chocolate boutiques in Palermo, specialty chocolate shops, and gourmet markets.

Whether you're drawn to the rhythmic beats of tango, the elegance of Argentine leather, or the flavors of artisanal chocolates, Buenos Aires offers a diverse array of souvenirs to suit every taste. Each keepsake carries a piece of the city's soul, ensuring that your memories of Buenos Aires endure long after your visit. Happy souvenir hunting!

Chapter 8

Cultural immersion

Tango: The Soul of Buenos Aires

Buenos Aires, often referred to as the "Paris of South America," is a city that pulsates with the rhythmic heartbeat of tango. This iconic dance form is more than just a series of steps; it's an integral part of the city's cultural identity, weaving through its streets, parks, and vibrant neighborhoods. Let's delve into the profound connection between Buenos Aires and tango, exploring its history, cultural significance, and the enduring allure that makes it the soul of the city.

1. The Origins: A Dance Born on the Margins

- Development: Tango originated in the working-class neighborhoods, or "conventillos," of Buenos Aires in the late 19th century. It was a fusion of African, European, and indigenous influences, creating a dance that reflected the diverse cultural tapestry of the city.
- Early Stages: Initially considered controversial and danced in the outskirts of society, tango was a raw and passionate expression of the struggles and joys of the urban poor.

2. Golden Age: The Roaring Twenties

- International Recognition: In the 1920s and 1930s, tango transcended its humble beginnings, gaining international acclaim and becoming a symbol of Argentina worldwide.
- Orchestras and Legends: Legendary figures like Carlos Gardel and Astor Piazzolla emerged, contributing to the

evolution of tango music. Orchestras, such as those led by Juan D'Arienzo and Aníbal Troilo, defined the Golden Age of Tango.

3. Tango Lyrics: Poetry of the Streets

- Narratives of Life: Tango lyrics are a poignant reflection of the city's stories, capturing the essence of love, loss, nostalgia, and the everyday struggles of Porteño life (life in Buenos Aires).
- Notable Tangos: Songs like "La Cumparsita," "El Choclo," and "Por Una Cabeza" have become timeless classics, transcending generations.

4. Dance: A Conversation Between Souls

- Passion and Connection: Tango is a dance of intense emotion and connection, where partners communicate through intricate steps, pauses, and close embraces.
- Milongas: The social dance gatherings known as milongas are integral to the tango scene. They occur in venues ranging from traditional clubs to open-air spaces, creating an inclusive environment for dancers of all skill levels.

5. Tango and Buenos Aires Today: A Living Tradition

- Street Performances: Tango can be witnessed in unexpected places, with street performers captivating passersby in parks, plazas, and iconic landmarks.
- Tango Shows: Buenos Aires boasts world-class tango shows, such as those in the historic neighborhoods of San Telmo and Abasto, offering immersive experiences that showcase the dance's dramatic flair.

6. Tango in Film and Literature: Immortalized on Screen and Page

- Cinema: Tango has left an indelible mark on Argentine cinema, with films like "The Tango Singer" and "Tango" capturing the dance's allure and complexity.
- Literary Inspirations: Numerous books, including Mario Benedetti's "Spring with a Broken Corner" and Jorge Luis Borges's poems, have drawn inspiration from the world of tango.

7. Tango Tourism: A Global Phenomenon

- Tango Festivals: Buenos Aires hosts tango festivals, attracting dancers and enthusiasts from around the globe. These events celebrate the dance's heritage and showcase its evolution.
- Tango Schools: Visitors can immerse themselves in tango through lessons offered by experienced instructors, providing an opportunity to learn the intricacies of this passionate dance.

8. Tango as Cultural Heritage: UNESCO Recognition

- Intangible Cultural Heritage: In 2009, UNESCO recognized the cultural significance of the tango by inscribing it on the Representative List of the Intangible Cultural Heritage of Humanity.
- Preserving Tradition: This acknowledgment highlights the importance of preserving and promoting tango as a living cultural expression.

Tango is more than a dance; it's an embodied narrative of Buenos Aires' soul. From its humble beginnings on the margins of society to its international acclaim, tango has evolved into a symbol of passion, resilience, and the intricate dance of life in the city. As you explore the streets of Buenos Aires, let the haunting melodies and evocative steps of tango guide you through the cultural heart of this vibrant South American metropolis. Tango isn't just a dance; it's the very heartbeat of Buenos Aires, echoing through its history, streets, and the hearts of those who call this city home.

Museums and Galleries of Buenos Aires

Buenos Aires, a city pulsating with cultural vibrancy, is home to a diverse array of museums and galleries that encapsulate the rich tapestry of Argentine history, art, and innovation. From world-class art collections to immersive cultural experiences, the city's cultural institutions invite visitors on a captivating journey through time and creativity. Here's a detailed exploration of the museums and galleries that make Buenos Aires a haven for art and history enthusiasts:

1. MALBA – Latin American Art Museum of Buenos Aires

The MALBA, Museo de Arte Latinoamericano de Buenos Aires, stands as a beacon for Latin American art. Located in the Palermo neighborhood, this museum showcases a superb collection of modern and contemporary art from across the region. Visitors can explore works by iconic artists such as Frida Kahlo, Diego Rivera, and Antonio Berni. The museum's commitment to fostering dialogue and understanding of Latin American art is evident in its diverse exhibitions, film screenings, and cultural events.

Highlights:

- Permanent Collection: Modern and contemporary Latin American art spanning the 20th and 21st centuries.

- Temporary Exhibitions: Rotating displays of cutting-edge artworks, exploring themes ranging from socio-political issues to avant-garde expressions.
- Cinema: MALBA regularly hosts film screenings, featuring a curated selection of Latin American cinema.

2. Museo Nacional de Bellas Artes (MNBA) – National Museum of Fine Arts

The MNBA, located in the Recoleta neighborhood, is Argentina's premier fine arts museum. Boasting an extensive collection that spans centuries and continents, the museum showcases European and Argentine art in a neoclassical building. From Renaissance masterpieces to 19th-century Argentine landscapes, the MNBA offers a comprehensive survey of artistic movements and styles.

Highlights:

- European Art: Works by Goya, El Greco, Van Gogh, and more.
- Argentine Art: A rich collection of paintings, sculptures, and decorative arts reflecting the evolution of Argentine artistic expression.
- Temporary Exhibitions: Rotating displays that complement the permanent collection, showcasing contemporary artists and thematic exhibitions.

3. Museo de Arte Contemporáneo de Buenos Aires (MACBA) – Museum of Contemporary Art of Buenos Aires

Located in the San Telmo neighborhood, MACBA focuses on contemporary art, offering a space for experimentation and innovation. The museum's minimalist architecture creates an immersive setting for visitors to engage with cutting-edge artworks. MACBA features both Argentine and international artists, contributing to the city's dynamic contemporary art scene.

Highlights:

- Contemporary Art: A diverse collection of contemporary works, including paintings, sculptures, and multimedia installations.
- Educational Programs: MACBA hosts workshops, lectures, and artist talks, fostering a dialogue between artists and the community.
- Public Programs: Engaging events such as film screenings, performances, and discussions that expand the museum experience beyond traditional exhibitions.

4. Museo Nacional de Arte Decorativo (MNAD) – National Museum of Decorative Arts

Housed in a French-style mansion in Recoleta, the MNAD is a testament to elegance and refinement. This museum offers a glimpse into the world of decorative arts, showcasing exquisite furniture, textiles, and objets d'art. The opulent surroundings provide a unique setting to appreciate the craftsmanship and design of various historical periods.

Highlights:

- Decorative Arts: A collection that spans from the Middle Ages to the 20th century, featuring European and Asian craftsmanship.
- Gardens: The museum's gardens are a serene oasis, offering a picturesque escape in the heart of the city.
- Special Exhibitions: Periodic exhibitions that delve into specific themes within the realm of decorative arts.

5. Museo Evita – Evita Museum

Dedicated to the life and legacy of Eva Perón, the Evita Museum provides an intimate look into the iconic figure's journey from actress to First Lady of Argentina. Housed in a historic building in Palermo, the museum features personal belongings, photographs, and multimedia exhibits that narrate Evita's impact on Argentine society.

Highlights:

- Personal Artifacts: Clothing, jewelry, and personal items belonging to Eva Perón.
- Interactive Displays: Multimedia exhibits and audiovisual presentations that bring Evita's story to life.
- Temporary Exhibitions: Periodic displays that explore different facets of Eva Perón's life and historical context.

6. Fundación Proa – Proa Foundation

Situated in the vibrant La Boca neighborhood, Fundación Proa is a contemporary art space that embraces experimentation and innovation. The museum, housed in a striking modern building, hosts a dynamic range of exhibitions featuring emerging and established artists from around the world.

Highlights:

- Contemporary Art Exhibitions: Rotating displays that showcase a diverse array of artistic expressions, from visual arts to multimedia installations.
- Café Proa: The museum's café offers panoramic views of the neighborhood and the Riachuelo River, creating a unique dining experience.

- Educational Programs: Workshops, talks, and cultural activities that engage the community in the exploration of contemporary art.

7. Museo de Arte Moderno de Buenos Aires (MAMBA) – Museum of Modern Art of Buenos Aires

MAMBA, located in San Telmo, is dedicated to modern and contemporary Argentine art. The museum's collection spans the 20th century to the present, highlighting the evolution of artistic movements in Argentina. MAMBA's commitment to fostering dialogue and inclusivity is evident in its diverse exhibitions and community engagement initiatives.

Highlights:

- Modern and Contemporary Argentine Art: A comprehensive collection that includes works by influential Argentine artists.
- Experimental Art: MAMBA often features experimental and avant-garde exhibitions that push the boundaries of artistic expression.
- Educational Programs: Workshops, lectures, and events that encourage active participation in the arts.

8. Museo Nacional de Arte Oriental (MNAO) – National Museum of Oriental Art

Tucked away in the Retiro neighborhood, the MNAO is a hidden gem dedicated to Asian art and culture. The museum's collection includes artifacts from China, Japan, India, and other Asian regions, providing a unique opportunity to explore the diverse artistic traditions of the East.

Highlights:

- Asian Art Collections: Ceramics, textiles, sculptures, and paintings representing various periods and styles.
- Japanese Garden: The museum is located adjacent to the beautiful Buenos Aires Japanese Gardens, creating a serene cultural enclave.
- Cultural Events: MNAO hosts events, workshops, and festivals that celebrate Asian culture and traditions.

9. Espacio de Arte Contemporáneo (EAC) – Contemporary Art Space

Housed in a former tobacco factory in the La Boca neighborhood, EAC is a dynamic contemporary art space that celebrates artistic experimentation. The industrial setting provides a unique backdrop for exhibitions and installations, fostering a dialogue between art and architecture.

Highlights:

- Site-Specific Installations: EAC often features large-scale, site-specific artworks that interact with the industrial features of the space.
- Emerging Artists: The space is a platform for emerging artists to showcase their work and engage with the local community.
- Open-Air Events: EAC hosts outdoor events, performances, and cultural gatherings that contribute to the neighborhood's artistic vitality.

10. Centro Cultural Kirchner (CCK) – Kirchner Cultural Center

Housed in the historic post office building, the CCK is a vast cultural complex dedicated to the performing arts, visual arts, and cultural events. This center is a hub for creativity and expression, hosting a wide range of activities that reflect Argentina's cultural diversity.

Highlights:

- Concert Halls: The CCK features concert halls, theaters, and exhibition spaces, providing a platform for musicians, dancers, and artists.
- Visual Arts Exhibitions: The center regularly hosts visual arts exhibitions, showcasing the work of contemporary artists.
- Educational Programs: Workshops, lectures, and cultural programs that engage audiences of all ages in the arts.

Exploring the museums and galleries of Buenos Aires is a journey into the heart and soul of Argentine culture. From the classical elegance of the National Museum of Fine Arts to the avant-garde expressions at the Contemporary Art Space, each institution offers a unique perspective, contributing to the city's vibrant cultural mosaic. Whether you're an art aficionado, history buff, or simply curious about Buenos Aires' creative spirit, these museums and galleries invite you to immerse yourself in the captivating world of Argentine art and culture.

Performing Arts in Buenos Aires

Buenos Aires, the cultural capital of Argentina, is a city where the performing arts take center stage, captivating audiences with a rich tapestry of expression, creativity, and diverse artistic forms. From the passion of tango to the elegance of classical music, and the avant-garde experiments in contemporary theater, Buenos Aires offers a dynamic and thriving performing arts scene that reflects the city's vibrant spirit. Let's delve into the various facets of performing arts that contribute to the cultural mosaic of Buenos Aires.

1. Tango: The Dance of Passion

- Milongas and Tango Houses: Tango, the iconic dance of Buenos Aires, is not just a cultural phenomenon; it's a way of life. Milongas, or tango dance halls, are scattered across the city, inviting locals and visitors to immerse themselves in the passionate embrace of this dance.
- Tango Houses: Renowned tango houses like Café de los Angelitos and El Querandí offer spectacular shows where the sensuality and drama of tango come to life on stage.

2. Classical Music: Elegance and Symphonic Beauty

- Teatro Colón: The Teatro Colón stands as one of the world's premier opera houses, hosting symphonies, operas, and ballets. Its acoustics and opulent architecture provide a sublime setting for classical music enthusiasts.
- Orchestras and Ensembles: Buenos Aires is home to esteemed orchestras like the Buenos Aires Philharmonic Orchestra and chamber ensembles that celebrate the works of classical composers.

3. Theater: A Stage for Innovation

- Avant-Garde Productions: The theater scene in Buenos Aires is marked by its diversity, with traditional theaters like Teatro Cervantes coexisting with experimental spaces like Timbre 4. Avant-garde productions explore themes ranging from political commentary to existential questioning.

- International Festivals: The city hosts international theater festivals, such as the Festival Internacional de Buenos Aires (FIBA), providing a platform for innovative performances from around the world.

4. Ballet and Dance: Grace in Motion

- Ballet Argentino: The Ballet Argentino, directed by acclaimed dancer Julio Bocca, showcases the elegance and virtuosity of Argentine dancers. Performances range from classical ballets to contemporary choreography.
- Dance Companies: Buenos Aires boasts a vibrant contemporary dance scene, with companies like Compañía Contemporánea and Compañía Nacional de Danza offering cutting-edge performances.

5. Cinema: A Visual Symphony

- Film Festivals: Buenos Aires hosts prestigious film festivals, including the Buenos Aires International Festival of Independent Cinema (BAFICI), celebrating the art of filmmaking. The city's cinemas screen a mix of international and Argentine films.
- Cinephile Culture: The city's cinephile culture extends beyond festivals, with independent cinemas like El Cultural San Martín and Cine Cosmos-Uba showcasing a diverse range of films.

6. Street Performances: Art in Public Spaces

- Plazas and Parks: The city's plazas and parks come alive with street performances, ranging from impromptu tango dances to theatrical interventions. These spontaneous

expressions contribute to the lively and communal atmosphere of Buenos Aires.
- Art in Transit: Public spaces like the Metrovías Subte feature art installations and performances, turning daily commutes into artistic experiences.

7. Contemporary Arts Centers: Hubs of Creativity

- Centro Cultural Kirchner: This cultural center housed in a former post office is a hub for the arts, hosting a diverse range of performances, exhibitions, and events. It is a symbol of Argentina's commitment to fostering creativity.
- Ciudad Cultural Konex: Known for its alternative and interdisciplinary events, Ciudad Cultural Konex is a dynamic space where performing arts, music, and visual arts converge.

8. Folk and Indigenous Performances: Celebrating Diversity

- Peñas: Folk music enthusiasts can experience traditional Argentine music in peñas, intimate venues where musicians perform heartfelt folk tunes. Venues like **La** Peña del Colorado showcase the soulful sounds of traditional genres.
- Indigenous Performances: Events like the Fiesta Nacional de la Vendimia celebrate indigenous cultures through dance, music, and rituals, offering a glimpse into Argentina's diverse heritage.

9. Street Art: Urban Canvases of Expression

- Murals and Performances: Buenos Aires is renowned for its vibrant street art scene. Street artists not only create visually stunning murals but also engage in live art

performances, adding a dynamic element to the city's urban landscape.
- Urban Interventions: Festivals like Meeting of Styles bring together street artists from around the world, turning the city into an ever-evolving canvas of expression.

Buenos Aires, with its pulsating artistic energy, celebrates the performing arts as an integral part of its cultural identity. From the passion of tango to the symphonic elegance of classical music, the avant-garde experiments in theater, and the dynamic expressions in dance and street art, Buenos Aires is a city that invites both locals and visitors to immerse themselves in a kaleidoscope of artistic experiences. As you wander through its theaters, dance halls, and public spaces, you'll discover that Buenos Aires is not just a city; it's a living canvas where the performing arts breathe life into its streets and resonate with the heartbeat of its people.

Walls of Expression: Buenos Aires' Street Art Scene Unveiled

Buenos Aires, a city that pulsates with creativity and cultural vibrancy, is renowned for its dynamic street art scene. From vibrant murals to politically charged stencils, the city's walls serve as a canvas for expression, reflecting the diverse voices and narratives that shape Argentine society. Here's a detailed exploration of Buenos Aires' captivating street art scene:

1. A Living Open-Air Gallery

- Overview: Buenos Aires is often hailed as one of the world's street art capitals, and for good reason. The city's streets, alleys, and building facades transform into a living, breathing gallery where artists use urban spaces as their canvases. From the bustling neighborhoods of Palermo and San Telmo to the historic cobblestone streets of La Boca, every corner unveils a new piece of art waiting to be discovered.

- Diversity of Styles: The street art scene in Buenos Aires is characterized by its diversity of styles, ranging from large-scale murals and colorful graffiti to detailed stencils and thought-provoking paste-ups. Artists draw inspiration from a myriad of sources, including indigenous cultures, political movements, and the city's own complex history.

2. Barrio of the Painted Walls: La Boca

- Overview: La Boca, a neighborhood steeped in history and known for its colorful houses, stands out as a hub for street art in Buenos Aires. Caminito Street, a vibrant pedestrian alley, serves as an open-air museum where artists showcase their talents on building facades and makeshift galleries. La Boca's street art tells stories of the neighborhood's working-class roots, tango culture, and the resilience of its people.

Highlights:

- El Caminito: A picturesque street where artists use the walls to depict scenes of everyday life, tango dancers, and historical figures.
- Local Identity: Street art in La Boca often reflects the neighborhood's identity and the struggles of its residents.

3. Palermo: Where Urban Art Meets Trendy Vibes

- Overview: Palermo, a trendy and eclectic neighborhood, seamlessly blends its vibrant street art scene with its fashionable boutiques and hip cafes. The walls of Palermo are adorned with large-scale murals, abstract compositions, and intricate designs that add a modern and artistic flair to the area. Palermo's street art reflects the neighborhood's dynamic and ever-evolving character.

- Street Art Tours: Visitors can immerse themselves in Palermo's street art by joining guided street art tours that provide insights into the artists, techniques, and cultural context of the vibrant murals.

4. Political Murals: A Visual Protest

- Overview: Buenos Aires' street art has a strong political undertone, serving as a platform for social and political commentary. Political murals can be found across the city, conveying messages of resistance, activism, and remembrance. From powerful portraits of political figures to depictions of social movements, these murals give voice to the city's history of activism and resilience.

- Memorial Walls: Some of the political murals serve as memorials to those who have fought for social justice, human rights, and political freedoms. These walls become poignant reminders of Argentina's turbulent past and ongoing struggles.

5. Artist Collectives and Collaborations

- Overview: Buenos Aires' street art scene is fostered by a sense of community and collaboration among artists. Various collectives and crews come together to create collaborative murals that showcase a blend of styles and perspectives. The collaborative nature of street art in

Buenos Aires encourages artists to share ideas, techniques, and spaces, creating a rich tapestry of creativity.
- Festivals and Events: Street art festivals and events, such as the Meeting of Styles, provide platforms for artists to collaborate on large-scale murals, transforming neighborhoods into dynamic art installations.

6. San Telmo: Bohemian Vibes and Artistic Corners

- Overview: San Telmo, known for its bohemian atmosphere and historic charm, is also home to an array of captivating street art. The narrow streets and colonial buildings serve as backdrops for colorful murals, hidden gems, and thought-provoking stencils. San Telmo's street art scene complements the neighborhood's artistic spirit and its role as a haven for creatives.
- Artistic Corners: Artists often utilize hidden corners, building facades, and even abandoned spaces in San Telmo to create unexpected and delightful art pieces that surprise and captivate passersby.

7. Evolving Canvases: Abandoned Spaces

- Overview: Abandoned buildings, warehouses, and factories provide unique canvases for street artists to unleash their creativity. These spaces, often transformed into vibrant art installations, contribute to the ever-changing landscape of Buenos Aires' street art scene. Abandoned spaces become both a playground and a gallery for artists to experiment with new styles and concepts.
- Urban Renewal: Street art plays a role in the urban renewal of neglected areas, transforming them into visually

engaging spaces that attract attention and bring communities together.

8. Interactive Street Art: Engaging the Community

- Overview: Some street art pieces in Buenos Aires go beyond mere visual appeal—they invite interaction and engagement from the community. Interactive murals encourage viewers to become part of the artwork, whether through optical illusions, participatory installations, or elements that respond to movement. These pieces add an extra layer of connection between the art and the people.
- Optical Illusions: Artists often play with perspective and optical illusions to create dynamic and interactive murals that change as viewers move around them.

9. Legal Walls and Permits

- Overview: While some street art in Buenos Aires is created without official permission, the city also provides spaces known as "legal walls" where artists can paint with the proper permits. These designated areas contribute to the organized development of the street art scene, allowing artists to express themselves in approved locations.
- Street Art Festivals: Events like the International Meeting of Styles and the Buenos Aires Ciudad Emergente Festival provide legal spaces for artists to create large-scale murals, fostering a positive relationship between the city and the street art community.

10. Emerging Talent: Nurturing Future Artists

- Overview: Buenos Aires' street art scene serves as a platform for emerging talent to gain recognition and visibility. Young artists, inspired by the city's rich cultural tapestry, contribute fresh perspectives and styles to the urban landscape. Street art becomes a form of cultural dialogue, allowing artists to communicate with the public and each other.

- Workshops and Mentorship: Various initiatives and workshops aim to nurture the next generation of street artists, providing them with skills, guidance, and opportunities to showcase their work in the public domain.

Exploring Buenos Aires' street art scene is a dynamic and ever-changing experience that invites visitors to engage with the city's cultural heartbeat. From the historical narratives in La Boca to the trendy murals of Palermo, each neighborhood tells a unique story through its walls. Buenos Aires' street art scene is not just about aesthetics; it's a living, breathing testament to the city's resilience, creativity, and the voices of its people.

A Cultural Mosaic of People and Language

Buenos Aires, the vibrant capital of Argentina, is a city that proudly wears the mantle of a cultural mosaic. Its streets, neighborhoods, and the very essence of daily life reflect a rich tapestry woven from the diverse threads of people and languages. Let's embark on a comprehensive exploration of the cultural diversity that defines Buenos Aires, from the myriad faces in its neighborhoods to the linguistic melodies that echo through its corridors.

People: A Tapestry of Faces and Heritage

Buenos Aires, often referred to as the "Paris of South America," is not just a city; it's a vibrant tapestry woven from the diverse faces and heritage of its people. The term "Porteños," used to describe the residents of Buenos Aires, encapsulates the city's unique cultural identity. Let's delve deeper into the intricate threads that make up this tapestry, celebrating the warmth, diversity, and rich heritage of the people who call Buenos Aires home.

Porteños: The Heartbeat of Buenos Aires

- Warm Hospitality: Porteños are renowned for their warm and welcoming nature. Whether you're navigating the bustling streets of Microcentro or strolling through the bohemian lanes of San Telmo, you'll encounter the friendly smiles and open hearts of the city's inhabitants.
- Passionate Nature: The people of Buenos Aires are passionate about life, love, and their city. This passion is palpable in every aspect of daily life, from the animated conversations in cafes to the fiery steps of a tango dance.

Diverse Origins: An Ancestral Melting Pot

- European Influence: Buenos Aires has a strong European influence, particularly from Italy and Spain. The waves of Italian and Spanish immigrants who arrived in the late 19th and early 20th centuries have left an indelible mark on the city's culture, cuisine, and traditions.
- Indigenous Roots: Beyond European ancestry, many Porteños proudly trace their roots to Argentina's indigenous populations. This connection to the land and its original inhabitants is reflected in cultural practices, art, and celebrations.

Cultural Influences: A Fusion of Traditions

- Italian Heritage: The Italian community has played a pivotal role in shaping Buenos Aires. This influence is evident in the city's love for pizza, pasta, and the ritual of gathering around the table for a shared meal. Italian surnames often pepper the city's phone books and business directories.
- Spanish Roots: Spanish colonial history is embedded in the architecture and language of Buenos Aires. The city's grand plazas, historical buildings, and the Spanish language spoken with a distinctive Argentine accent reflect a deep connection to Spain.

Afro-Argentine Legacy: Celebrating Diversity

- La Boca: A Cultural Hub: La Boca, a neighborhood known for its colorful houses and vibrant street art, also celebrates its Afro-Argentine roots. The legacy of African influence is visible in the local music, dance, and cultural festivals that honor the contributions of the Afro-Argentine community.
- Candombe Rhythms: Candombe, a rhythmic and percussive musical style, originated in the African communities of Buenos Aires. Today, it continues to be a vital part of the city's cultural fabric, with drumming circles and performances adding a lively beat to festivals and events.

Jewish Community: A Rich Cultural Thread

- Once: The Heart of Jewish Buenos Aires: The Once neighborhood is a focal point for Buenos Aires' Jewish community. Synagogues, kosher markets, and cultural institutions thrive in this area, contributing to the city's cultural and religious diversity.

- Cultural Contributions: The Jewish community has made significant contributions to Buenos Aires' cultural landscape, from literature to film. Festivals and events celebrating Jewish heritage are integral to the city's cultural calendar.

Languages: A Linguistic Melting Pot in Buenos Aires

Buenos Aires, a city known for its rich cultural diversity, is also a linguistic melting pot where the cadence of conversation echoes with unique accents, expressions, and linguistic nuances. The Spanish language, deeply rooted in the city's history, is spoken with a distinct Argentine flair. However, Buenos Aires' linguistic landscape goes beyond Spanish, incorporating a variety of elements that contribute to the city's vibrant and eclectic verbal tapestry.

1. Argentine Spanish: A Distinctive Accent

- Vos vs. Tú: One of the most noticeable features of Argentine Spanish is the use of "vos" instead of the more common "tú" for the second person singular. This linguistic choice adds a distinctive touch to daily conversations, creating a sense of familiarity and friendliness.
- Unique Pronunciation: The Argentine accent, often referred to as Rioplatense Spanish, carries its own pronunciation variations. Porteños, the residents of Buenos Aires, are known for their melodic and rhythmic way of speaking.

2. Lunfardo: A Playful and Colorful Slang

- Origins and Evolution: Lunfardo is a unique slang that originated in the working-class neighborhoods of Buenos Aires in the late 19th century. It was initially a secret code

used by criminals and marginalized communities, but over time, it became an integral part of everyday speech.
- Incorporation into Daily Language: Lunfardo incorporates words and expressions from Italian, Spanish, and indigenous languages. It adds a playful and colorful dimension to conversations, making Buenos Aires' speech truly distinctive.

3. Bilingualism: English Influence

- Educational Emphasis: English is widely taught in schools, and many Porteños are bilingual, especially in business and academic settings. The emphasis on bilingual education reflects the city's global outlook and the importance of English in international communication.
- Code-Switching: It's not uncommon to hear Porteños seamlessly switch between Spanish and English in the same conversation, showcasing the city's linguistic flexibility.

4. Italian Legacy: Linguistic Echoes

- Italian Influence: The significant Italian immigrant population that settled in Buenos Aires has left a lasting linguistic legacy. Italian words and expressions are often incorporated into everyday language, particularly in culinary terms and family settings.
- Expressions of Identity: The use of Italian words is not just linguistic; it's a reflection of the cultural identity and heritage of many Porteños with Italian roots.

5. Indigenous Languages: Preserving Heritage

- Recognition of Indigenous Roots: While Spanish is the dominant language, there is a growing recognition and

appreciation for Argentina's indigenous languages. Efforts are made to preserve and revitalize languages such as Quechua and Mapudungun, acknowledging the country's diverse indigenous heritage.
- Cultural Celebrations: Indigenous languages are often featured in cultural events, festivals, and educational initiatives, promoting linguistic diversity and cultural understanding.

6. Multilingualism: Embracing Diversity

- International Influence: Buenos Aires, as a global city, attracts a diverse population, including expatriates and international students. This diversity contributes to the city's multilingual environment, where you may encounter conversations in languages ranging from Portuguese to French.
- Cultural Exchange: The multilingualism of Buenos Aires fosters cultural exchange and enriches the city's social fabric. It's not uncommon to find language exchange meet-ups and events where people come together to practice and celebrate linguistic diversity.

7. Sign Language: Inclusion and Accessibility

- Accessibility Initiatives: Buenos Aires has made strides in promoting inclusivity, including initiatives to make public spaces more accessible for individuals with hearing impairments. Argentine Sign Language (Lengua de Señas Argentina - LSA) is an essential part of the city's commitment to accessibility.
- Educational Integration: Efforts are made to integrate sign language into educational settings, ensuring that the

linguistic needs of the deaf and hard-of-hearing community are recognized and accommodated.

Buenos Aires' linguistic melting pot is not just a collection of words; it's a vibrant symphony that reflects the city's cultural richness and diverse heritage. From the rhythmic cadence of Argentine Spanish to the playful expressions of Lunfardo and the echoes of other languages, the linguistic landscape of Buenos Aires is a testament to the city's openness, adaptability, and embrace of cultural diversity. As you navigate the streets, engage in conversations, and immerse yourself in the cultural tapestry of Buenos Aires, you'll discover that language is not just a means of communication; it's a dynamic and integral part of the city's identity and soul.

Festivals and Events That Define Buenos Aires' Cultural Landscape

Buenos Aires, a city that dances to the rhythm of cultural diversity and artistic fervor, hosts a myriad of festivals and events throughout the year. From traditional celebrations rooted in Argentine history to avant-garde cultural happenings that push the boundaries of creativity, Buenos Aires is a stage where the vibrant spirit of the city comes to life. Here's a detailed exploration of the cultural festivals and events that shape the cultural landscape of Buenos Aires:

1. Feria de Mataderos: A Folkloric Fiesta

- Overview: Feria de Mataderos, held in the neighborhood of the same name, is a folkloric festival that celebrates Argentina's rural traditions. This vibrant fair showcases traditional dances, music, and crafts, allowing visitors to immerse themselves in the rich cultural heritage of the Argentine countryside.

Highlights:

- Traditional Gastronomy: Sample regional dishes and traditional Argentine barbecue.
- Live Folk Performances: Enjoy live music, folk dances, and performances by local artists.
- Crafts Fair: Browse through a diverse array of handmade crafts and artisanal products.

2. Buenos Aires International Independent Film Festival (BAFICI)

- Overview: BAFICI is one of the most significant film festivals in Latin America, showcasing independent and avant-garde films from around the world. Held annually, this festival transforms Buenos Aires into a cinematic hub, attracting filmmakers, industry professionals, and cinephiles.

Highlights:

- International Films: Screenings of cutting-edge independent films from various genres and countries.
- Directorial Debuts: BAFICI often features debut films and emerging talents in the world of cinema.
- Q&A Sessions: Engage with filmmakers and industry experts through post-screening discussions and panels.

3. Tango Buenos Aires Festival and World Cup

- Overview: As the birthplace of tango, Buenos Aires pays homage to this iconic dance form through the Tango Buenos Aires Festival and World Cup. This event brings together tango enthusiasts, dancers, and musicians from around the globe for a celebration of the passionate and intricate art of tango.

Highlights:

- Tango Competitions: Witness world-class tango dancers compete for the prestigious title.
- Live Performances: Enjoy electrifying live performances by renowned tango musicians and orchestras.
- Dance Workshops: Participate in tango workshops to learn the steps and techniques from master instructors.

4. La Noche de los Museos: Night of Museums

- Overview: La Noche de los Museos is an annual event that transforms Buenos Aires into a citywide museum celebration. On this night, museums, galleries, and cultural institutions open their doors to the public for free, offering a unique opportunity to explore the city's cultural treasures after dark.

Highlights:

- Cultural Immersion: Experience art, history, and culture as you explore museums and galleries throughout the city.
- Special Exhibitions: Museums often host special exhibitions, live performances, and interactive installations.
- Nighttime Atmosphere: The city comes alive with a festive atmosphere, as people of all ages engage in cultural exploration.

5. Ciudad Emergente: Emerging Culture Festival

- Overview: Ciudad Emergente is a dynamic festival that spotlights emerging talents in various artistic disciplines, including music, film, literature, and visual arts. This event provides a platform for young and innovative artists to showcase their work and connect with a broader audience.

Highlights:

- Live Performances: Enjoy live music concerts featuring emerging bands and solo artists.
- Art Installations: Experience interactive art installations and exhibitions by up-and-coming visual artists.
- Literary Events: Engage with young authors and participate in literary discussions and book presentations.

6. Buenos Aires Jazz Festival

- Overview: The Buenos Aires Jazz Festival is a celebration of jazz that attracts musicians, enthusiasts, and jazz aficionados from around the world. This annual event features an eclectic lineup of performances, ranging from traditional jazz to avant-garde improvisation.

Highlights:

- International Jazz Acts: Experience performances by acclaimed jazz artists and bands from various countries.
- Jam Sessions: Join in or witness spontaneous jam sessions that bring musicians together in creative collaborations.
- Workshops and Masterclasses: Learn about jazz history, theory, and technique through educational programs led by seasoned musicians.

7. Carnival Porteño: Buenos Aires Carnival

- Overview: Carnival Porteño, Buenos Aires' carnival celebration, is a lively and colorful extravaganza that takes place in various neighborhoods across the city. This festive event brings together music, dance, and vibrant costumes, creating a dynamic and joyous atmosphere.

Highlights:

- Parades: Enjoy vibrant parades featuring elaborately decorated floats, dancers, and musical performances.
- Murga Groups: Experience the rhythmic beats and lively dances of murga groups, a traditional form of Argentine street theater.
- Street Parties: Join in the street parties where locals and visitors come together to celebrate with music and dance.

8. Buenos Aires Book Fair (Feria del Libro)

- Overview: The Buenos Aires Book Fair is one of the largest literary events in the Spanish-speaking world. Held annually, this fair brings together authors, publishers, and book lovers for a celebration of literature and intellectual exchange.

Highlights:

- Author Presentations: Attend book presentations, readings, and discussions with renowned authors.
- Book Exhibitions: Explore a vast array of books from various genres, including literature, poetry, and non-fiction.
- Cultural Talks: Engage in cultural talks and debates on literature, philosophy, and current affairs.

9. Festival Internacional de Buenos Aires (FIBA): International Theater Festival

- Overview: FIBA is an international theater festival that showcases a diverse range of theatrical performances, including plays, experimental theater, and contemporary dance. The festival attracts theater enthusiasts, artists, and performers from different corners of the globe.

Highlights:

- International Performances: Experience cutting-edge theater productions from renowned international companies.
- Experimental Works: FIBA often features avant-garde and experimental performances that challenge traditional notions of theater.
- Workshops and Seminars: Engage in workshops and discussions with theater professionals and artists.

10. Festival and World Championship of Tango for People with Disabilities

- Overview: This unique and inclusive festival highlights the universal nature of tango by bringing together dancers with disabilities from around the world. The Festival and World Championship of Tango for People with Disabilities aims to showcase the accessibility and adaptability of tango as a dance form.

Highlights:

- Inclusive Performances: Witness captivating tango performances by dancers with various abilities.

- Workshops: Participate in inclusive tango workshops that promote accessibility and inclusivity.
- Global Participation: Dancers from different countries come together to celebrate the diversity of tango.

Buenos Aires' cultural festivals and events paint a vibrant portrait of a city that values creativity, diversity, and the arts. Whether you're drawn to the rhythmic beats of tango, the intellectual stimulation of a book fair, or the cinematic magic of an international film festival, Buenos Aires offers a kaleidoscope of cultural experiences throughout the year. These festivals not only showcase the city's rich cultural heritage but also serve as platforms for innovation, inclusivity, and the celebration of artistic expression.

Local Customs and Etiquette in Buenos Aires

Buenos Aires, with its rich cultural tapestry, is a city that values tradition, hospitality, and a genuine connection with others. Understanding local customs and etiquette is not only a sign of respect but also an invitation to fully immerse yourself in the unique charm of the Porteño way of life. Here's a comprehensive guide to local customs and etiquette in Buenos Aires:

1. Warm Greetings and Social Kisses

- Social Kisses: One of the most distinctive customs in Buenos Aires is the greeting with a kiss on the cheek (beso). When meeting friends or acquaintances, expect one or two kisses on the right cheek. It's a warm and friendly gesture that signifies closeness.

2. Relaxed Approach to Time

- Punctuality: While business meetings often adhere to a strict schedule, social gatherings and casual events tend to follow a more relaxed sense of time. It's not uncommon for people to arrive a bit late, and patience is appreciated.

3. Engaging in Small Talk

- Politeness in Conversation: Porteños value politeness in conversations. Engaging in small talk before diving into business or personal matters is customary. Asking about someone's day or expressing interest in their well-being is a common practice.

4. Appreciating Mate Culture

- Sharing Mate: Mate is a traditional Argentine herbal tea, and sharing it is a communal and social activity. If someone offers you mate, it's a gesture of friendship. Sipping from the shared mate cup and passing it back is a symbol of camaraderie.

5. Respecting Personal Space

- Comfortable Proximity: Porteños are generally comfortable with close physical proximity during conversations. It's common to stand closer to someone than in many Western cultures. Respect personal space but be prepared for a closer conversational style.

6. Dress Stylishly and Appropriately

- Smart Casual: Buenos Aires is a stylish city, and locals often take pride in their appearance. While casual attire is acceptable in many situations, dressing well is appreciated, especially when attending cultural events, upscale restaurants, or social gatherings.

7. Tipping and Service Expectations

- Tipping Culture: Tipping is customary in Buenos Aires, and it's generally expected to leave a tip of around 10% in restaurants. In taxis, rounding up the fare is common. Tipping service staff, such as porters and housekeeping, is also appreciated.

8. Dining Etiquette

- Late Dinners: Dinner in Buenos Aires is a leisurely affair and often starts later than in many other cultures. It's not uncommon for locals to dine around 9 PM or later. Reservations are recommended for popular restaurants.
- Sharing Dishes: Sharing dishes is common in Argentine dining culture. Large portions are often meant to be shared among the table, contributing to a communal and convivial atmosphere.

9. Respecting Tango Traditions

- Respectful Observation: Tango is more than a dance in Buenos Aires; it's a cultural treasure. When watching a tango performance, maintain a respectful silence, and applaud at appropriate times. Avoid talking or distracting the performers.

10. Friendship and Loyalty

- Building Trust: Porteños value deep and lasting friendships. Building trust and demonstrating loyalty are essential in cultivating meaningful connections. Once trust is established, friendships often endure for a lifetime.

11. Navigating Social Hierarchy

- Formality in Business: In business settings, maintaining a level of formality is crucial. Titles and proper greetings are important. Addressing someone by their title and last name initially is a sign of respect until a more familiar relationship is established.

12. Celebrating National Holidays

- Cultural Pride: Argentines take great pride in their national identity, and national holidays are celebrated with enthusiasm. Participate in local festivities, parades, and events to witness the deep-rooted cultural pride of the Porteños.

13. Respecting Cultural Diversity

- Cultural Sensitivity: Buenos Aires is a melting pot of cultures, and respecting this diversity is essential. Be open-minded, embrace different traditions, and avoid making assumptions based on stereotypes. Engaging with various cultural aspects enriches your experience.

14. Gracious Hosts and Guests

- Hospitality: Porteños are known for their hospitality, and being a gracious host or guest is highly valued. If invited to someone's home, bringing a small gift or a bottle of wine is a thoughtful gesture. Expressing gratitude for hospitality is equally important.

15. Understanding Local Gestures

- Gesture Language: Porteños often use hand gestures to express themselves. While some gestures may be universal, others are culturally specific. Observing and learning about these gestures can help you navigate conversations more effectively.

As you navigate the streets of Buenos Aires, remember that local customs and etiquette are not just formalities but the heartbeat of Porteño culture. Embracing these traditions opens doors to genuine connections, cultural insights, and a more immersive experience in the dynamic and welcoming city of Buenos Aires. Whether sharing mate with new friends, enjoying a late-night dinner, or watching a passionate tango performance, embracing the local way of life is the key to unlocking the true spirit of Buenos Aires.

Chapter 9

Nightlife and Entertainment

Unveiling Buenos Aires' Bars and Pubs

Embark on a journey through Buenos Aires' eclectic and vibrant nightlife, where each bar and pub unveils a unique facet of the city's culture. From historic haunts to trendy mixology hubs, discover the top recommendations that promise unforgettable nights in Buenos Aires.

1. Bar El Federal: A Timeless Haven in San Telmo

Address: Carlos Calvo 599, San Telmo

Overview:

- Nestled in the heart of San Telmo, Bar El Federal stands as a timeless icon that transports visitors to a bygone era. Dating back to 1864, this historic bar exudes a classic charm with its wooden interiors, antique mirrors, and a long bar that invites patrons to linger over a drink. The ambience resonates with the spirit of the neighborhood, making it a beloved haunt for locals and tourists alike.

Top Recommendations:

- Classic Argentine Cocktails: Savor the essence of Argentine libations with time-tested classics like the Fernet and Coke or the refreshing Clericó.
- Artistic Ambiance: Immerse yourself in the bohemian atmosphere as you admire the eclectic artwork adorning the

walls, a testament to the bar's longstanding cultural significance.
- Live Music Evenings: Experience the soulful melodies of live tango performances that grace the intimate space on selected evenings.

2. Frank's Bar: A Speakeasy Gem in Palermo

Address: Arévalo 1443, Palermo

Overview:

- Step into the clandestine world of Frank's Bar, a speakeasy hidden behind an unassuming door in the Palermo district. With an ambiance that harks back to the Prohibition era, this intimate establishment offers a journey through time. Dark wood, dim lighting, and a hint of mystery set the stage for an evening of crafted cocktails and secretive conversations.

Top Recommendations:

- Secretive Entrance: Enter through a phone booth within a sandwich shop to access the hidden world of Frank's, adding an element of intrigue to your night out.
- Crafted Cocktails: Indulge in expertly crafted cocktails that blend international mixology trends with Argentine flavors, showcasing the skill of the talented bartenders.
- Jazz Nights: Enjoy the enchanting allure of live jazz performances that grace the cozy space, enhancing the sophisticated yet relaxed atmosphere.

3. La Puerta Roja: Where Art and Libations Converge in San Telmo

Address: Chacabuco 733, San Telmo

Overview:

- La Puerta Roja, translating to "The Red Door," beckons patrons into an artistic haven in the heart of San Telmo. The vibrant pub seamlessly combines live music, contemporary art, and a laid-back atmosphere. The walls adorned with murals and paintings create an immersive experience, making it a popular spot for those seeking a blend of culture and cocktails.

Top Recommendations:

- Artistic Ambiance: Immerse yourself in the ever-evolving art installations that grace the walls, contributing to the dynamic and creative atmosphere.
- Craft Beer Selection: Explore a diverse range of craft beers, both local and international, as La Puerta Roja takes pride in offering a selection that caters to beer enthusiasts.
- Live Music Sessions: Delight in the live music sessions featuring local bands and artists, creating a lively and engaging backdrop for your evening.

4. El Preferido de Palermo: A Rustic Retreat in La Boca

Address: Jorge Luis Borges 2108, Palermo

Overview:

- Transport yourself to the rustic charm of El Preferido de Palermo, a traditional pulpería nestled in the trendy Palermo neighborhood. This historic tavern preserves the essence of Argentine folklore, providing a cozy retreat where patrons can revel in the warmth of wood-paneled interiors and the nostalgic allure of vintage décor.

Top Recommendations:

- Argentine Wine Selection: Explore the extensive collection of Argentine wines, curated to showcase the rich viticulture of the region, complementing the hearty Argentine cuisine.
- Traditional Pulpería Fare: Indulge in traditional Argentine dishes such as empanadas, milanesa, and choripán, prepared with an authentic touch.
- Live Folk Performances: Experience the soulful melodies of live folk performances, a tribute to Argentina's musical roots, held on select evenings.

5. Florería Atlántico: A Multi-Sensory Marvel in Recoleta

Address: Arroyo 872, Recoleta

Overview:

- Florería Atlántico transcends the conventional bar experience, offering a multi-sensory journey that combines mixology, gastronomy, and a touch of maritime mystique. Concealed behind the façade of a flower shop, this speakeasy invites patrons to descend into a subterranean world where creativity knows no bounds.

Top Recommendations:

- Gastronomic Cocktails: Delight in innovative cocktails that incorporate elements of Argentine cuisine, creating a fusion of flavors that captivates the palate.

- Clandestine Atmosphere: Revel in the clandestine ambiance, surrounded by nautical-inspired décor, vintage maps, and an authentic submarine entrance.
- Seafood Specialties: Pair your libations with a selection of fresh and delectable seafood dishes, elevating the culinary experience to new heights.

6. Milion: Palatial Grandeur in Retiro

Address: Paraná 1048, Retiro

Overview:

- Milion stands as a testament to the grandeur of Buenos Aires' architectural heritage, housed in a stunning French-style mansion in the Retiro district. This sophisticated bar seamlessly blends historic elegance with contemporary style, offering an opulent setting for an evening of refined indulgence.

Top Recommendations:

- Elegant Rooftop Terrace: Ascend to the rooftop terrace adorned with lush greenery and vintage furnishings, providing a luxurious backdrop for panoramic views of the city.
- Exquisite Cocktail Menu: Explore an extensive cocktail menu featuring signature concoctions and classic libations, each crafted with precision and flair.
- Live Jazz Evenings: Immerse yourself in the enchanting ambiance of live jazz performances that grace the opulent interiors, enhancing the sophisticated atmosphere.

7. Gibraltar: British Flair in San Telmo

Address: Peru 895, San Telmo

Overview:

- Gibraltar, a piece of Britain nestled in San Telmo, captures the essence of a traditional British pub in the heart of Buenos Aires. With its cozy interiors, wooden furnishings, and a welcoming atmosphere, this pub invites patrons to experience the warmth of British hospitality while enjoying a diverse range of libations.

Top Recommendations:

- British Pub Fare: Indulge in classic British pub fare, including hearty pies, fish and chips, and a selection of ales that pay homage to the pub's cultural roots.
- Craft Beer Selection: Explore a curated collection of craft beers, featuring both local and international brews, providing a diverse range of options for beer enthusiasts.
- Pub Quiz Nights: Engage in the lively atmosphere of pub quiz nights, a popular event that adds an interactive and convivial element to the pub experience.

8. Antares Brewery: Craft Beer Haven in Palermo

Address: Armenia 1447, Palermo

Overview:

- For aficionados of craft beer, Antares Brewery in Palermo stands as a mecca of hops and malts. Boasting a laid-back and friendly ambiance, this brewery offers a diverse range of house-brewed beers, providing a refreshing alternative to traditional Argentine libations.

Top Recommendations:

- Craft Beer Tasting: Embark on a tasting journey with Antares' extensive selection of craft beers, ranging from hoppy IPAs to rich stouts, allowing patrons to explore the nuances of each brew.
- Beer and Food Pairing: Enhance your beer experience by pairing it with a selection of delectable dishes, crafted to complement the flavors of the brewery's diverse beer offerings.
- Lively Beer Garden: Enjoy the casual and convivial atmosphere of the beer garden, where locals and visitors alike come together to savor the pleasures of craft beer.

9. Victoria Brown Bar: Industrial Chic in Palermo Hollywood

Address: Costa Rica 4827, Palermo Hollywood

Overview:

- Victoria Brown Bar, nestled in the trendy Palermo Hollywood district, captivates with its industrial-chic aesthetics and an ambiance that seamlessly blends sophistication with a touch of edginess. This bar, hidden behind an unassuming door, offers a contemporary setting for those seeking a stylish and upscale nightlife experience.

Top Recommendations:

- Innovative Mixology: Immerse yourself in the world of innovative mixology, with a menu featuring avant-garde cocktails that push the boundaries of flavor and presentation.
- Exclusive Atmosphere: Revel in the exclusivity of the bar's atmosphere, where sleek interiors, dim lighting, and a

curated selection of music contribute to an intimate and stylish setting.
- Signature Brownie Martini: Indulge in the bar's signature Brownie Martini, a delectable concoction that combines the richness of chocolate with the kick of premium vodka.

10. Rey de Copas: A Regal Retreat in Recoleta

Address: Vicente López 1750, Recoleta

Overview:

- Rey de Copas, translating to "King of Cups," lives up to its regal name by offering an elegant and refined space in the upscale Recoleta neighborhood. This lounge bar, adorned with plush furnishings and soft lighting, invites patrons to unwind in an ambiance of sophistication and luxury.

Top Recommendations:

- Signature Cocktails: Delight in the bar's signature cocktails, where skilled mixologists craft libations that balance creativity with timeless appeal.
- Cigar Lounge Experience: Experience the luxury of the cigar lounge, where connoisseurs and enthusiasts can savor premium cigars paired with exquisite spirits in an intimate and exclusive setting.
- Live DJ Sets: Enjoy the curated sounds of live DJ sets that add a rhythmic and energetic dimension to the elegant atmosphere, creating a perfect backdrop for an upscale night out.

Buenos Aires' bars and pubs are not merely places to sip on libations; they are portals to the city's soul. Each establishment, with its unique ambiance, crafted cocktails, and cultural resonance, adds a layer to the intricate tapestry of Buenos Aires' nightlife. Whether you find yourself in the historic corners of San Telmo, the trendy landscapes of Palermo, or the refined atmosphere of Recoleta, the city's bars and pubs invite you to partake in a celebration of Argentine culture, one drink at a time.

Live Music Venues in Buenos Aires

Buenos Aires, a city pulsating with rhythm and passion, offers an unparalleled live music scene that reflects the diverse cultural influences woven into its fabric. From intimate tango bars to lively jazz clubs, the city is a haven for music enthusiasts seeking an authentic and soul-stirring experience. Here are top recommendations for live music venues where you can immerse yourself in the melodic heartbeat of Buenos Aires.

1. La Trastienda: Where Music Comes Alive

Genre Diversity: La Trastienda is a legendary venue that has hosted a myriad of musical genres, from rock and pop to tango and electronic. Its intimate setting allows for a close connection between performers and the audience.

Historic Significance: With a history dating back to the 1990s, La Trastienda has become an iconic space that continues to attract both local and international artists.

2. Café Vinilo: A Haven for Jazz Enthusiasts

Jazz Jams and Performances: Café Vinilo is a cozy venue in Palermo dedicated to jazz, hosting regular jam sessions and performances by local and international jazz musicians. The warm ambiance and acoustics make it a favorite among jazz enthusiasts.

Eclectic Programming: Beyond jazz, Café Vinilo occasionally features other genres, ensuring a diverse musical experience for its audience.

3. Niceto Club: Electric Vibes and Eclectic Acts

Vibrant Nightlife: Niceto Club is a dynamic venue in Palermo that caters to diverse tastes, featuring live music ranging from indie and electronic to rock and pop. Its energetic atmosphere and vibrant crowd make it a hotspot for those looking to dance the night away.

Eclectic Acts: The venue hosts both emerging local bands and well-established international acts, creating a platform for musical exploration.

4. La Viruta: Tango, Dance, and Cultural Fusion

Tango Nights: La Viruta, located in the basement of the Armenian Cultural Center, is a tango haven where locals and visitors come together to dance and enjoy live tango music. The venue offers tango classes, creating a community of tango enthusiasts.

Cultural Fusion: Beyond tango, La Viruta occasionally features live music from other genres, showcasing the venue's commitment to cultural fusion.

5. Thelonious Club: Jazz Excellence in San Telmo

Dedicated to Jazz: Thelonious Club, named after jazz legend Thelonious Monk, is a gem in San Telmo for jazz aficionados. The club has a cozy and intimate setting, providing an ideal space to appreciate the nuances of live jazz performances.

Late-Night Sessions: Thelonious Club is renowned for its late-night jam sessions, where both established and emerging jazz musicians gather to create spontaneous and captivating musical moments.

6. La Tramoya: Intimate Acoustic Experiences

Acoustic Settings: La Tramoya, located in the heart of San Telmo, is an intimate venue known for its acoustic performances. From solo artists to small ensembles, the focus here is on creating an up-close and personal connection between musicians and the audience.

Local Talent: La Tramoya often showcases local talent, providing a platform for emerging artists to share their music in an inviting and laid-back atmosphere.

7. Notorious: Jazz, Blues, and Beyond

Musical Variety: Notorious, situated in the Palermo neighborhood, is a cultural space that hosts live music events spanning jazz, blues, rock, and more. The venue's eclectic programming ensures a diverse range of musical experiences for attendees.

Cultural Hub: Beyond live music, Notorious is a cultural hub that hosts book presentations, art exhibitions, and other events, making it a well-rounded destination for those seeking a cultural immersion.

8. La Biblioteca Café: A Literary and Musical Oasis

Literary-Musical Fusion: La Biblioteca Café seamlessly blends literature and music, creating a unique space where bookshelves meet stages. The venue hosts live music events, including jazz and bossa nova, providing a serene ambiance for both literary and musical exploration.

Sunday Jazz Brunch: La Biblioteca Café is famous for its Sunday Jazz Brunch, where patrons can enjoy live jazz performances alongside a delightful brunch menu.

9. Boris Club de Jazz: Elegance and Timeless Jazz

Classic Jazz Atmosphere: Boris Club de Jazz, located in the heart of Palermo, exudes an atmosphere of classic jazz elegance. The venue hosts live jazz performances, and its intimate setting allows for an immersive experience with the music.

Variety of Acts: From traditional jazz to contemporary interpretations, Boris Club de Jazz attracts a diverse range of jazz acts, ensuring a dynamic and ever-evolving musical calendar.

10. Club Atlético Fernández Fierro (CAFF): Avant-Garde Tango

Experimental Tango: Club Atlético Fernández Fierro, often referred to as CAFF, is a unique space in Almagro that specializes in avant-garde tango. The venue is a melting pot of musical experimentation, featuring unconventional tango performances that push the boundaries of the genre.

Community Spirit: CAFF is not just a venue; it's a community hub where tango enthusiasts come together to explore the innovative and experimental facets of this traditional Argentine dance form.

Buenos Aires' live music venues offer a symphony of sounds that resonate with the city's soul. Whether you're drawn to the passionate embrace of tango, the improvisational magic of jazz, or the energetic beats of rock and electronic music, Buenos Aires invites you to immerse yourself in a diverse and vibrant musical landscape. As you explore these top live music venues, you'll discover that each note played and each rhythm danced to is a testament to the city's rich cultural heritage and its enduring love affair with music.

Dancing into the Night: Buenos Aires' Nightclubs and Late-Night Tango Extravaganza

As the moon rises over Buenos Aires, the city comes alive with the pulsating beats of music, the twirls of dancers, and the vibrant energy of its nightclubs and late-night tango venues. In this exploration, we venture into the heart of Buenos Aires' nightlife, where nightclubs and the enchanting rhythms of tango converge to create an unforgettable nocturnal experience.

Late-Night Tango: A Soulful Dance Under the Stars

1. The Essence of Tango in Buenos Aires

Tango, the heartbeat of Buenos Aires, is not confined to daylight hours. As the city transitions into the night, the soulful strains of tango music echo through the streets, inviting both seasoned dancers and curious onlookers to engage in the intimate and passionate dance.

Milongas: Where Tango Comes to Life

- Milongas are social events or dance halls where tango aficionados gather to dance, socialize, and revel in the enchanting world of tango. These late-night gatherings are scattered across the city, each with its unique ambiance and character.

Highlighted Milongas:

- La Viruta (Armenia 1366, Palermo): A vibrant and welcoming milonga that hosts nightly tango sessions, attracting both beginners and seasoned dancers. La Viruta embraces a friendly atmosphere and offers tango lessons for those eager to join the dance floor.
- El Beso (Riobamba 416, Balvanera): Known as one of the oldest milongas in Buenos Aires, El Beso exudes a classic tango ambiance. With its traditional setting and live orchestras, it provides an authentic experience for tango enthusiasts.

2. Midnight Tango Shows: Theatrical Elegance Unveiled

For those seeking a more curated tango experience, Buenos Aires boasts a selection of midnight tango shows that blend artistry, music, and dance. These shows are often hosted in historic venues, offering a glimpse into the golden era of tango while captivating audiences with modern interpretations.

Esquina Carlos Gardel (Carlos Gardel 3200, Abasto):

- This iconic venue, named after the legendary tango singer Carlos Gardel, invites patrons to an evening of sophistication and nostalgia. The venue's architecture and decor transport visitors to the glamorous 1930s, while the live tango performances showcase the artistry and passion of this beloved dance form.

Café de los Angelitos (Av. Rivadavia 2100, Congreso):

- Stepping into Café de los Angelitos feels like entering a time capsule of tango's glory days. This historic venue, with its opulent interiors and live orchestras, hosts midnight tango shows that combine traditional choreography with contemporary flair. The intimate setting allows guests to immerse themselves in the world of tango up close.

Nightclubs: Where the Beat Never Stops

1. Buenos Aires' Nightclub Scene: A Tapestry of Rhythms

As the night deepens, Buenos Aires' nightclub scene comes to life, offering a diverse range of music genres, dance floors, and immersive experiences. From electronic beats to Latin rhythms, the city's nightclubs cater to a broad spectrum of musical tastes.

Crobar (Marcelino Freyre s/n, Palermo):

- Crobar, nestled in the heart of Palermo, stands as a pillar of Buenos Aires' electronic music scene. With its cutting-edge sound system and renowned guest DJs, Crobar attracts electronic music enthusiasts from around the city. The expansive dance floor, illuminated by pulsating lights, creates an electrifying atmosphere that persists until the early morning hours.

Pacha Buenos Aires (Av. Rafael Obligado 6151, Costanera):

- A global nightlife brand, Pacha Buenos Aires brings the party to the shores of the Rio de la Plata. This waterfront nightclub is renowned for its lively atmosphere, international DJ lineups, and an eclectic mix of electronic and Latin beats. The outdoor terrace provides panoramic views of the river, adding an extra layer of allure to the Pacha experience.

2. Latin Beats and Sizzling Dance Floors

Buenos Aires' nightclubs aren't just limited to electronic music; they also embrace the vibrant rhythms of Latin America. From salsa and reggaeton to cumbia and bachata, these venues invite patrons to dance the night away to the infectious beats of Latin music.

La Trastienda (Balcarce 460, San Telmo):

- La Trastienda transcends the traditional nightclub concept, offering a versatile space that hosts live Latin music performances, dance parties, and cultural events. With its intimate setting and eclectic programming, La Trastienda creates a dynamic atmosphere where patrons can immerse themselves in the richness of Latin sounds.

Niceto Club (Niceto Vega 5510, Palermo):

- Niceto Club stands as a pillar of Buenos Aires' alternative music scene, embracing a diverse range of genres, including Latin beats. This iconic venue hosts themed parties, live music shows, and DJ sets that cater to a broad audience. The pulsating dance floor, adorned with vibrant visuals, ensures an energetic and unforgettable night out.

Insider Tips: Navigating the Nightlife Landscape

1. Dress Codes and Entrance Policies

- Nightclubs and tango shows in Buenos Aires often adhere to specific dress codes, ranging from casual chic to formal attire. It's advisable to check the venue's requirements before heading out to ensure a seamless entrance. Some upscale venues may also have age restrictions or entrance fees, particularly on special event nights.

2. Tango Etiquette for Late-Night Milongas

- For those venturing into the late-night milonga scene, understanding tango etiquette is essential. While many milongas welcome beginners, it's courteous to observe the dance floor dynamics before joining in. Inviting someone to dance is done traditionally through a cabeceo, a subtle nod or glance, and respecting each dancer's space and rhythm is paramount.

3. Transportation Considerations

- Given the late-night nature of Buenos Aires' nightlife, it's essential to plan transportation accordingly. While some neighborhoods are easily navigable on foot, others may require taxis or rideshare services. It's advisable to choose well-lit and reputable transportation options, especially if exploring less familiar areas.

Buenos Aires' nightlife, with its amalgamation of tango rhythms and pulsating beats in nightclubs, offers an immersive and diverse experience for nocturnal adventurers. Whether losing oneself in the passionate embrace of tango under the stars or dancing until dawn in a vibrant nightclub, the city's nightlife is a symphony that resonates with the soul of Buenos Aires.

Chapter 10

Practical Tips for Travelers

Navigating Buenos Aires Safely

As you embark on your journey through the vibrant streets of Buenos Aires, ensuring your safety and well-being becomes a top priority. This comprehensive guide provides a detailed overview of safety guidelines, offering valuable insights to help you navigate the city with confidence and peace of mind.

1. General Safety Tips

Stay Informed About Local Conditions

- Before exploring Buenos Aires, stay informed about current local conditions, weather forecasts, and any potential safety concerns. Utilize reliable travel resources, check official websites, and consider registering with your embassy for travel advisories.

Use Reputable Transportation Services

- Opt for reputable transportation services, such as registered taxis, rideshare apps, or official public transportation. Avoid accepting rides from unmarked vehicles and ensure that the vehicle you choose has proper identification.

Secure Your Belongings

- Keep your belongings secure to prevent theft. Use anti-theft backpacks or money belts for valuables, and be cautious with your personal items in crowded places. Avoid displaying expensive jewelry and electronics openly.

Emergency Contacts and Local Services

- Save emergency contact numbers, including local authorities and your country's embassy, in your phone. Familiarize yourself with the location of hospitals, police stations, and other essential services in the areas you plan to visit.

2. Personal Safety in Public Spaces

Be Aware of Your Surroundings

- Maintain situational awareness in public spaces. Be conscious of your surroundings, especially in crowded areas and tourist attractions. Avoid distractions such as excessive use of mobile phones while walking.

Walk in Well-Lit Areas at Night

- If you're exploring the city at night, stick to well-lit and populated areas. Avoid poorly lit streets and alleys. Consider using transportation services, even for short distances, during late hours.

Be Cautious with Strangers

- While Buenos Aires is generally friendly, exercise caution with strangers. Be wary of unsolicited assistance, and avoid engaging in conversations that make you uncomfortable. Trust your instincts.

3. Health and Safety Measures

Health Precautions

- Stay hydrated, especially during warm weather, and be cautious with street food. Ensure your vaccinations are up-to-date and carry any necessary medications. In case of illness, seek medical assistance promptly.

Sun Protection

- Buenos Aires can experience intense sunlight. Use sunscreen, wear a hat, and stay hydrated to protect yourself from the sun. If you plan to be outdoors for an extended period, consider carrying a reusable water bottle.

COVID-19 Safety Measures

- Adhere to local COVID-19 safety guidelines and regulations. This may include wearing masks in crowded places, maintaining social distancing, and following any specific protocols outlined by authorities. Stay informed about vaccination requirements and testing facilities.

4. Money and Financial Safety

Use Reliable ATMs and Currency Exchange Services

- Choose ATMs located in well-trafficked areas and affiliated with reputable banks. Be cautious with currency exchange services, and avoid unauthorized or street exchanges. Keep a record of your card details and emergency contact numbers.

Split Your Valuables

- Divide your money, cards, and valuables between different pockets or pouches. This way, you minimize the risk of losing all your valuables in case of theft. Consider using a travel money belt for added security.

5. Local Customs and Etiquette

Respect Local Customs

- Familiarize yourself with local customs and etiquette. Respect cultural norms, particularly in religious sites and traditional neighborhoods. Learn a few basic phrases in Spanish to enhance communication and show appreciation for the local culture.

Dress Modestly When Appropriate

- In certain areas, particularly religious sites and more conservative neighborhoods, dressing modestly is appreciated. Be mindful of local dress codes, and adjust your attire accordingly.

6. Nightlife Safety Measures

Travel in Groups

- If you're enjoying the nightlife, travel in groups when possible. Avoid isolated areas, and be cautious when accepting drinks from strangers. Trust your instincts, and have a plan for getting back to your accommodation safely.

Inform Someone of Your Plans

- Let someone know your plans for the evening, including your destination and expected return time. This ensures that someone is aware of your whereabouts, enhancing your safety.

7. Local Laws and Regulations

Familiarize Yourself with Local Laws

- Understand and respect local laws and regulations. Be aware of any specific rules regarding photography, public behavior, and prohibited substances. Ignorance of the law is not an excuse.

Document Copies

- Keep copies of important documents, including your passport, ID, and travel insurance. Store these separately from the originals to facilitate replacement in case of loss or theft.

8. Emergency Preparedness

Emergency Evacuation Plan

- Have an emergency evacuation plan, especially if you're staying in a hotel or accommodation. Familiarize yourself with escape routes and emergency exits.

Travel Insurance

- Invest in comprehensive travel insurance that covers medical emergencies, trip cancellations, and theft. Confirm the details of your coverage and keep a copy of your policy in a secure location.

By adhering to these safety guidelines, you're well-equipped to make the most of your time in Buenos Aires. Embrace the rich culture, explore the diverse neighborhoods, and savor the vibrant nightlife with the assurance that your safety remains a top priority. Buenos Aires awaits, promising a memorable and secure experience for every traveler.

Essential Spanish Phrases

Embarking on a journey to Buenos Aires is not only a feast for the senses but also an opportunity to immerse yourself in the local language and culture. While many Porteños (Buenos Aires locals) are welcoming and accommodating, having a few essential Spanish phrases at your disposal can enhance your experience and make communication smoother. Here's a comprehensive guide to basic phrases that will prove invaluable during your stay in Buenos Aires:

Greetings and Politeness:

- Hello / Hi: Hola
- Good morning: Buenos días
- Good afternoon / Good evening: Buenas tardes
- Good night: Buenas noches
- How are you?: ¿Cómo estás? (informal) / ¿Cómo está? (formal)
- Please: Por favor
- Thank you: Gracias
- You're welcome: De nada
- Excuse me / Sorry: Perdón / Disculpe (formal)

Introductions:

- My name is...: Mi nombre es...
- What's your name?: ¿Cómo te llamas? (informal) / ¿Cómo se llama usted? (formal)

Common Courtesies:

- Yes: Sí
- No: No
- Please, thank you, and excuse me go a long way: Por favor, gracias, perdón.

Navigating Conversations:

- I don't understand: No entiendo
- Can you help me?: ¿Puede ayudarme?
- I'm lost: Estoy perdido/a
- Where is...?: ¿Dónde está...?

Dining and Ordering:

- I would like...: Me gustaría...
- The bill, please: La cuenta, por favor
- Menu: Menú
- Water: Agua
- Coffee: Café
- Wine: Vino
- Delicious: Delicioso/a

Getting Around:

- Where is the bathroom?: ¿Dónde está el baño?
- How much is this?: ¿Cuánto cuesta esto?
- I need a taxi: Necesito un taxi
- Airport: Aeropuerto
- Bus station: Estación de autobuses

Shopping:

- How much does this cost?: ¿Cuánto cuesta esto?
- I'll take it: Lo/la/los/las compro
- Do you have change?: ¿Tiene cambio?

Emergencies:

- Help!: ¡Ayuda!
- I need a doctor: Necesito un médico

- Emergency services (police, ambulance, fire): Emergencias (policía, ambulancia, bomberos)

Numbers:

- 1: Uno
- 2: Dos
- 3: Tres
- 4: Cuatro
- 5: Cinco
- 10: Diez
- 20: Veinte
- 50: Cincuenta
- 100: Cien

Basic Expressions:

- Yes, please: Sí, por favor
- No, thank you: No, gracias
- I'm sorry: Lo siento
- Good luck: Buena suerte
- Cheers!: ¡Salud!

Armed with these essential phrases, you're well-equipped to navigate the charming streets of Buenos Aires and engage with the locals on a more personal level. Language is a powerful bridge that connects cultures, and as you explore the vibrant tapestry of Buenos Aires, these basic Spanish expressions will not only facilitate communication but also open doors to enriching cultural experiences. ¡Buena suerte! (Good luck!)

Health and Medical Services in Buenos Aires

Ensuring your health and well-being is paramount while exploring the dynamic streets of Buenos Aires. This comprehensive guide provides detailed insights into health and medical services, equipping you with the knowledge to navigate any medical situation with confidence and ease.

1. Healthcare System Overview

Public Healthcare in Buenos Aires

- Buenos Aires boasts a robust healthcare system that includes public and private services. Public healthcare facilities, known as "hospitales" or "centros de salud," offer medical services to residents and tourists alike. While these facilities provide essential care, they may have longer wait times and limited English-speaking staff.

Private Healthcare Services

- Private healthcare in Buenos Aires is renowned for its quality and efficiency. Private hospitals, clinics, and medical centers offer a range of services, often with English-speaking staff. These establishments provide a higher level of comfort and faster service, making them an excellent choice for those seeking expedited and specialized care.

2. Finding Medical Assistance

Emergency Services

- In case of a medical emergency, dial 107 to reach emergency services in Buenos Aires. This number connects you to ambulances that can transport you to the nearest medical facility.

Pharmacies

- Pharmacies, known as "farmacias," are prevalent in Buenos Aires, and you can find them throughout the city. Pharmacists are usually knowledgeable and can provide assistance for minor ailments. For prescription medications, you'll need to visit a doctor.

Medical Centers and Hospitals

- For non-emergency medical issues, consider visiting medical centers or hospitals. Private hospitals, such as Hospital Alemán and Hospital Italiano, are well-regarded and have English-speaking staff. In emergencies, head to the nearest hospital for immediate assistance.

3. Travel Health Precautions

Vaccinations

- Ensure your routine vaccinations are up-to-date before traveling to Buenos Aires. Additionally, consider vaccinations for diseases such as Hepatitis A and B. Check with your healthcare provider for personalized advice based on your health and travel plans.

Water and Food Safety

- While tap water in Buenos Aires is generally safe to drink, some travelers prefer bottled water. Exercise caution with street food, and opt for well-cooked meals in established restaurants to reduce the risk of foodborne illnesses.

Altitude Considerations

- If you plan to travel to higher altitudes outside Buenos Aires, such as the Andes, be mindful of altitude sickness. Allow time for acclimatization, stay hydrated, and avoid excessive physical exertion.

4. Health Insurance and Medical Costs

Travel Insurance

- Before your trip, obtain comprehensive travel insurance that covers medical emergencies, including hospitalization and evacuation. Confirm the details of your coverage, and keep a copy of your insurance policy with you.

Payment for Medical Services

- In private healthcare facilities, payment is often required at the time of service. Acceptable forms of payment may include cash, credit cards, or international travel insurance. Ensure you have a means of payment readily available when seeking medical assistance.

5. English-Speaking Medical Professionals

Private Clinics and Hospitals

- Private clinics and hospitals in Buenos Aires often have English-speaking medical professionals. When making appointments, inquire about the availability of English-speaking staff to ensure effective communication.

Pharmacies and Assistance

- In major tourist areas, pharmacists and staff at larger establishments may speak English. Pharmacies in upscale neighborhoods and commercial districts are more likely to have English-speaking staff to assist you with medication and health-related queries.

6. Specialized Medical Services

Dental Care

- Buenos Aires offers quality dental care services. Private dental clinics are prevalent, and many dentists speak English. In case of a dental emergency, contact a dental clinic directly or seek assistance from your accommodation.

Optical Services

- For optical services, such as eye exams and prescription glasses, private optometry clinics and optical stores are widely available. Some clinics may have English-speaking staff to help you with your eye care needs.

7. Mental Health Support

Counseling and Therapy

- If you require mental health support, Buenos Aires has professionals offering counseling and therapy services. Some private clinics and healthcare facilities provide psychological support, and you can inquire about English-speaking therapists.

Emergency Mental Health Hotline

- For immediate assistance with mental health concerns, you can contact the emergency mental health hotline at 135.

This service connects you with professionals who can provide guidance and support.

By familiarizing yourself with the healthcare landscape in Buenos Aires, you empower yourself to navigate any health-related situation during your travels. Whether seeking routine medical care, emergency assistance, or specialized services, the city's healthcare infrastructure is well-equipped to address your needs. Prioritize your well-being, stay informed, and enjoy your exploration of Buenos Aires with confidence.

Chapter 11

Additional Resources for an Informed Journey

Embarking on a journey to Buenos Aires becomes even more enriching when armed with a wealth of information and resources. This comprehensive guide introduces additional resources to enhance your experience, providing valuable insights and tips to make the most of your time in this vibrant city.

1. Tourist Information Centers

Services Offered

- Tourist Information Centers are scattered across Buenos Aires, offering a wealth of resources for visitors. These centers provide maps, brochures, and helpful guides to navigate the city. Knowledgeable staff can assist with travel itineraries, recommend attractions, and provide insights into local culture.

Locations

- Major tourist areas, airports, and transportation hubs house these centers. Notable locations include Ezeiza International Airport, Jorge Newbery Airport, and key neighborhoods like Palermo and San Telmo.

2. Online Travel Portals

Comprehensive Travel Websites

- Explore comprehensive travel websites that delve into the heart of Buenos Aires. Platforms like Lonely Planet,

TripAdvisor, and Expedia offer city guides, travel forums, and user reviews, providing a diverse range of perspectives and recommendations.

Local Blogs and Travel Diaries

- Dive into the experiences of fellow travelers through local blogs and travel diaries. Bloggers often share hidden gems, personal anecdotes, and practical tips that may not be found in mainstream travel guides. Follow blogs like "Buenos Aires Local" for an insider's perspective.

3. Language Learning Apps

Spanish Language Apps

- While many in Buenos Aires speak English, learning some basic Spanish phrases can enhance your experience. Language learning apps like Duolingo and Babbel offer interactive lessons to help you grasp essential phrases for communication and cultural immersion.

Translation Apps

- For real-time translation assistance, consider apps like Google Translate. These apps can help bridge language barriers, making interactions with locals more enjoyable and enriching.

4. Local Events and Festivals Calendars

Cultural Events and Festivals

- Stay updated on local events and festivals by consulting online calendars and event listings. Websites like Time Out Buenos Aires and local event platforms showcase cultural happenings, festivals, and exhibitions, allowing you to immerse yourself in the city's dynamic cultural scene.

Tango Shows and Performances

- For those eager to experience Buenos Aires' renowned tango scene, check out dedicated platforms offering information on tango shows, milongas, and dance performances. Websites like Hoy Milonga provide event listings for tango enthusiasts.

5. Transportation Apps

Ride-Sharing Services

- Efficiently navigate Buenos Aires with ride-sharing services like Uber and Cabify. These apps offer a convenient and reliable means of transportation, especially in areas where taxis may be less accessible.

Public Transportation Apps

- Leverage public transportation apps to plan your routes and stay informed about bus and subway schedules. The "Cómo Llego" app is a valuable tool for navigating Buenos Aires' extensive public transportation network.

6. Safety Apps

Safety Alerts and Information

- Stay informed about safety updates and alerts through dedicated apps. Many cities, including Buenos Aires, have apps that provide real-time information on safety, traffic, and other relevant updates.

7. Social Media Platforms

Travel Communities

- Join travel communities and forums on platforms like Facebook and Reddit. Engage with fellow travelers, ask questions, and share your experiences. Local expat groups can also offer valuable insights and recommendations.

Instagram and Pinterest

- Visual platforms like Instagram and Pinterest are treasure troves of inspiration for exploring Buenos Aires. Search for location tags, travel hashtags, and curated boards to discover stunning visuals and hidden gems.

8. Currency Exchange Apps

Currency Conversion Apps

- Stay updated on currency exchange rates with apps like XE Currency or OANDA. These tools help you make informed financial decisions and ensure you receive fair rates when exchanging money.

9. Sustainable Travel Resources

Eco-Friendly Guides

- For eco-conscious travelers, explore sustainable travel guides and resources. Websites like Responsible Travel provide insights into environmentally friendly activities, accommodations, and practices in Buenos Aires.

Bike-Sharing Apps

- Discover the city at your own pace with bike-sharing apps. Buenos Aires has a robust bike-sharing system, and apps like BA Ecobici can help you locate bike stations and plan your cycling routes.

10. Local Culinary Guides

Food and Culinary Apps

- Explore Buenos Aires' diverse culinary scene with food and restaurant apps. Platforms like TheFork and TripAdvisor offer reviews, ratings, and recommendations for local eateries, ensuring a delightful gastronomic journey.

Cooking Classes and Food Tours

- Immerse yourself in Argentine cuisine by joining cooking classes or food tours. Check out platforms like Airbnb Experiences for authentic culinary experiences led by local chefs and food enthusiasts.

11. Weather Apps

Real-Time Weather Updates

- Stay informed about the weather conditions during your stay with reliable weather apps. AccuWeather and The Weather Channel provide real-time updates, ensuring you're prepared for any changes in weather.

12. Cultural Etiquette Guides

Understanding Local Customs

- Enhance your cultural experience by familiarizing yourself with local customs and etiquette. Cultural etiquette guides, available online or in travel books, provide valuable insights into Argentine social norms and traditions.

13. Local Art and Museum Apps

Virtual Museum Tours

- Explore Buenos Aires' rich cultural heritage through virtual museum tours. Many museums and art galleries offer online experiences, allowing you to appreciate the city's artistic treasures from the comfort of your device.

14. Music and Entertainment Platforms

Local Music Streaming Apps

- Discover the sounds of Buenos Aires with local music streaming apps. Platforms like Spotify and local music apps showcase the city's diverse music scene, from traditional tango to contemporary Latin beats.

Event Listings for Concerts and Performances

- Stay informed about live music events, concerts, and performances by checking event listings on platforms like Bandsintown. These apps ensure you don't miss out on the vibrant music scene in Buenos Aires.

15. Volunteer and Community Engagement Resources

Volunteering Opportunities

- For those interested in giving back to the community, explore volunteer opportunities in Buenos Aires. Websites like Volunteer World and Idealist provide information on local initiatives and organizations seeking assistance.

Community Events and Initiatives

- Stay connected with local communities and social initiatives by attending community events. Websites like Meetup and local community calendars offer insights into gatherings, workshops, and collaborative projects.

Arming yourself with these additional resources enhances your journey through Buenos Aires. From local insights and cultural guides to practical apps for transportation and safety, these resources empower you to create a memorable and well-informed experience in one of South America's most captivating cities.

Chapter 12

Conclusion

Reflecting on Your Buenos Aires Experience

As your journey through Buenos Aires draws to a close, take a moment to reflect on the rich tapestry of experiences, flavors, and encounters that have unfolded in this vibrant city. Buenos Aires, with its distinctive blend of history, culture, and warmth, has likely left an indelible mark on your memories.

- Cultural Immersion: The cultural immersion in Buenos Aires goes beyond the tangible landmarks and iconic sites. It's the rhythm of tango echoing through the cobblestone streets, the taste of traditional Argentine cuisine, the warmth of the people, and the nuanced conversations that create a mosaic of experiences.
- Connections Made: Perhaps you've shared a mate with locals, danced the night away in a tango club, or engaged in heartfelt conversations with new friends. These connections, woven into the fabric of your journey, are the threads that make Buenos Aires more than a destination—it becomes a part of your story.
- Navigating Diversity: Navigating the city's diverse neighborhoods, embracing local customs, and savoring the unique blend of languages and accents, you've witnessed the kaleidoscope of Buenos Aires' identity. The city's ability to seamlessly blend tradition with modernity is a testament to its dynamic spirit.
- Personal Growth: Traveling is not just about exploring new places; it's a journey of personal growth and discovery.

Buenos Aires, with its open arms and inviting culture, has likely challenged, inspired, and broadened your perspective, fostering a deeper understanding of the world and yourself.

Inviting You Back to Argentina

As you bid farewell to Buenos Aires, consider this not as an end but as an invitation to return. Argentina, with its vast landscapes, diverse cities, and rich cultural heritage, has much more to offer. From the breathtaking landscapes of Patagonia to the cultural richness of Cordoba and the wines of Mendoza, Argentina is a country that beckons you to explore further.

- Discovering More Regions: Each region of Argentina unfolds its own unique charm. Explore the Andean landscapes of Salta, traverse the scenic routes of the Lake District, or marvel at the Iguazu Falls in the north. Argentina's geographical diversity promises a kaleidoscope of experiences waiting to be discovered.
- Culinary Delights: Beyond Buenos Aires, each province boasts its own culinary delights. Indulge in the traditional dishes of the north, such as empanadas and humita, or savor the world-class wines of Mendoza. Argentina's gastronomic landscape is as diverse as its geography.
- Festivals and Celebrations: Argentina's calendar is dotted with vibrant festivals and celebrations. Whether it's the energetic Carnival in Gualeguaychú, the cultural extravaganza of the National Grape Harvest Festival in Mendoza, or the traditional folklore celebrations, each event offers a unique window into the country's soul.

- Adventure Awaits: For the adventurous soul, Argentina presents a playground of outdoor activities. Embark on a trek in Patagonia, ride the rapids in Bariloche, or explore the surreal landscapes of the Puna. The possibilities for adventure in Argentina are as boundless as its horizons.
- Cultural Depth: Argentina's cultural depth extends beyond Buenos Aires. Delve into the indigenous heritage in the northwest, visit Jesuit missions in Cordoba, or experience the gaucho way of life on the pampas. Each region contributes to the multifaceted mosaic of Argentine culture.

In conclusion, as you carry the memories of Buenos Aires with you, remember that Argentina, with its vast and diverse landscapes, awaits your return. The warmth of the people, the passion of the tango, and the cultural richness of this South American gem will be here to welcome you back whenever you choose to rediscover its wonders. Until then, may your travels be filled with new adventures and the enduring spirit of Buenos Aires accompany you wherever you go. ¡Hasta la próxima! (Until next time!)

Printed in Great Britain
by Amazon